New and Different Materials for Weaving and Coiling

Marianne Barnes

4880 Lower Valley Road · Atglen, Pennsylvania 19310

Other Schiffer Books on Related Subjects:
Antler Art for Baskets and Gourds. Betsey Sloan.
    ISBN: 978-0-7643-3615-7. $19.99
Coiled Designs for Gourd Art. Catherine Devine.
    ISBN: 978-0-7643-3011-7. $14.99
Creating Bottles with Gourds and Fiber. Jim Widess.
    ISBN: 978-0-7643-3866-3. $19.99
Creating Gourd Birds with the Fairy Gourdmother®. Sammie Crawford.
    ISBN: 978-0-7643-3735-2. $24.99
Decorating Gourds: Carving, Burning, Painting, and More. Sue Waters.
    ISBN: 978-0-7643-1312-7. $14.99
Gourd Art Basics: The Complete Guide to Cleaning, Preparation and Repair. C. Angela Mohr.
    ISBN: 978-0-7643-2829-9. $14.99

Schiffer Books are available at special discounts for bulk purchases for sales promotions or premiums. Special editions, including personalized covers, corporate imprints, and excerpts can be created in large quantities for special needs. For more information contact the publisher:

Published by Schiffer Publishing Ltd.
4880 Lower Valley Road
Atglen, PA 19310
Phone: (610) 593-1777; Fax: (610) 593-2002
E-mail: Info@schifferbooks.com

For the largest selection of fine reference books on this and related subjects, please visit our website at **www.schifferbooks.com**
We are always looking for people to write books on new and related subjects. If you have an idea for a book, please contact us at proposals@schifferbooks.com

This book may be purchased from the publisher.
Include $5.00 for shipping.
Please try your bookstore first.
You may write for a free catalog.

In Europe, Schiffer books are distributed by
Bushwood Books
6 Marksbury Ave.
Kew Gardens
Surrey TW9 4JF England
Phone: 44 (0) 20 8392 8585;
Fax: 44 (0) 20 8392 9876
E-mail: info@bushwoodbooks.co.uk
Website: www.bushwoodbooks.co.uk

Designed by RoS
Type set in Helvetica/Humanist 521 BT

ISBN: 978-0-7643-3992-9
Printed in China

Dedication

This book is dedicated to my wonderful photographer, Kelly Hazel. She went with me on field trips and came every time I called her to photograph something. Her photography is awesome and makes my books look great! It is also dedicated to my wonderful husband, Jim, who is my main supporter and helper. I also dedicate this work to my mom, Christine, who has always encouraged my interest in the arts.

Acknowledgments

There are so many people I would like to thank for helping me write this book. First of all I want to thank Schiffer Publishing for the beautiful first book I wrote, *Weaving on Gourds*, and encouraging me to write this book about the materials used for weaving and coiling. I want to thank Cass Schorsch who not only sent information and photographs for this book, but helped me find some of the talented weavers who graciously agreed to help by sending information and photographs, tutorials, and patterns. To all who contributed to this book, I want to sincerely thank you for sharing your art with me so I could share it. I want to especially thank Nancy Basket, a wonderful friend and Native American artist. She allowed me to bring my photographer, Kelly, into her home and yard to photograph all her natural materials. She also shared much information for this book. I do need to acknowledge my good friends Becky and Sandy who proofread for me. Last of all, I am so honored to have been able to teach many classes throughout the years to basket weavers and gourd enthusiasts. Thanks for helping me grow and share what I have learned about weaving and gourds.

Contents

Introduction

There are so many materials that can be used both to weave and coil baskets and on gourds. While writing my first book, *Weaving on Gourds,* I was surprised to find weavers who use such a wide variety of materials—natural and manmade. So I decided to research some of these materials. To my amazement, I found out that I have many of these materials growing in my own yard and even found materials in my house. This book has a wealth of information about natural materials and other exciting resources like wire, paper, and recycled items. Maybe you will find some in your yard or house, too. I am not an expert on collecting and using natural materials, but I did a lot of research and tried many of the materials. I also have many friends who *do* work with naturals. I know that some of you may prepare your material differently or may have different names for the materials, especially the natural ones. As I researched, I saw many natural materials spelled differently and some of the information varied. If so, please let me know, as I am still learning.

I find the use of naturals so amazing. Some of the materials can be found all over the United States, but some are only found in localized areas. Much of the information on collecting and preparing the materials and where to find them was shared by some wonderful basket makers and gourd artists. You will find not only information about the materials but also some tutorials, a little history, and even some projects to try. Of course, I could not include all the materials that can be used for weaving and coiling because the list is quite extensive. Just about anything you can bend and manipulate can be used for weaving. I hope that what I have included will make you want to try some of the materials that are available to you and experiment with the weaving techniques. Many of the materials are available through suppliers, so I have included a list of weaving and gourd vendors in the book. You will also find an extensive gallery of baskets and gourds, so you can see all the weaving possibilities.

Nancy Basket's pond where she grows bulrush, horsetail, and many other plants for weaving. *Photography by Kelly Hazel.*

Naturals: seashells, shelf fungus, birch bark, philodendron sheath, walnut slices, sweet gum balls, bitternut hickory, pine needles, cedar bark, jacaranda pods, heart pod, dandelion stems, orchid tree pods, and sweetgrass. *Courtesy of Angie Wagner.*

Section One:

1

Materials

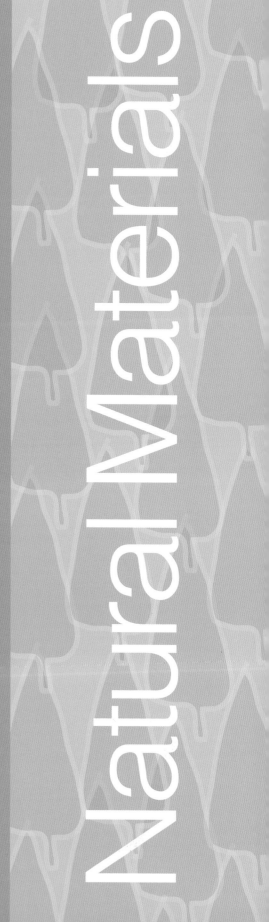

Natural Materials

1.1: A Little History

Weaving has been a long tradition in just about every country in the world. Baskets have been around for a long time. In earlier times in the United States handmade baskets were the most common objects found in every household. Baskets were made for a purpose. In fact, the name of the basket revealed its purpose: berry basket, market basket, feather basket, etc. Today baskets are purposeful or used for decoration.

The materials used for basket weaving in America depended on what was readily available. Native Americans and colonists discovered that basketry allowed them to take best advantage of the natural abundance available to them in the form of reeds, grass, straw, pine needles, roots, vines, corn shucks, and splints of willow, walnut, hickory, oak, and ash with a minimum of tools. Natural materials were the ones where you could go out, collect the materials, and prepare the basket. The style of baskets that were made depended on (1) the techniques that were passed down from generation to generation and (2) what type of vessel was needed. In the north, black and white ash trees were readily available. The ash baskets were first made by Native Americans. The Algonquin of the northeast made baskets using primarily black ash. The Shaker baskets, made of ash, originated in New York from techniques learned from the Algonquin Indians. Shaker baskets are still made today. In New England, sturdy double walled baskets were made for a variety of purposes, such as collecting fruits and vegetables and storing them in cellars. The open weave baskets were made for things like straining curds of cheese. The Native American Indians of the Pacific northwest used strips of spruce root and cedar bark to make their baskets. These materials were tightly twined or plaited to create the baskets. Nantucket basket making began in the 1800s. Men who worked on the lightships made these baskets using a wooden mold to create the shape. During the second half of the nineteenth century, men from the island of Nantucket often signed up for duty on the lightships that were stationed around the island. Many basket makers had a "production-line" that turned the bottoms, wove the staves, and finished the baskets while serving aboard the ship.

The whalers were thought to be the ones who first brought rattan in the form of cane to Nantucket, but according to some sources, rattan (used in "Nantucket" baskets) was widely introduced to America by Cyrus Wakefield, founder of Wakefield Rattan and Wicker Furniture, beginning around 1840. Rattan has become the primary material for weaving baskets today.

Nantucket style basket woven with cane and made by the author. *Photography by Kelly Hazel.*

Cherokee white oak basket in author's collection. Artist unknown. *Photography by Kelly Hazel.*

Gourd with woven pine needle base, made by Penny Reynolds. *Photography by Kelly Hazel.*

Earth Spirit Basket, 8 1/2" H x 9" W. Gourd with pyroengraved botanical design and woven with seagrass, coconut fiber, sisal, hemp, and wool. *Courtesy of Jaynie Barnes.*

In the southwest, the Hopi basket makers coiled tightly woven vessels using grasses, willow bark, and even devil's claw. They would sew bundles of yucca fibers in their baskets for decoration.

In the southeast, the Cherokee used river cane, white oak, and honeysuckle to make their baskets. They still use these materials today, but the materials are harder to find because of increasing population and growth in building and construction. White oak baskets in the south were made primarily by the men who cut the trees and prepared the splints. The baskets were crudely made and used for collecting products in the field.

The sweetgrass basket makers of South Carolina and coastal Georgia used sweetgrass, pine needles, and bulrush for coiling the baskets, and the leaves of the Palmetto palm tree for stitching. The baskets were first made by the African-American slaves and were made for use in the rice fields. These baskets were made of coils of bulrush and sewn with ash strips. Around the 1800s, the women started using sweetgrass sewn with strips of Palmetto leaves to make sewing baskets. The sweetgrass baskets are still made today and sold along the streets in Charleston and Mount Pleasant, South Carolina. The material is becoming harder to find and the basket makers have to travel further to find it. Hotels and developments are taking the land where the grass grew. This tradition has been passed down from one generation to another.

The last history I will mention will be from the Appalachia regions in the eastern part of the United States. This area was also called the Southern Highlands. The terrain was very rough and the people were primitive. The people made baskets to use in everyday life. They made them from easily accessible materials, such as willow, honeysuckle, rye, pine needles, straw, corn husks, and raffia. The primary baskets were made of white oak.

Weaving on gourds does not have the same history as baskets. Gourds were used, and still are used today, for many utilitarian purposes, such as utensils, containers, religious and ceremonial objects, musical instruments, and clothing or costumes. You can find information about gourds in the book by Ginger Summit, *Gourds in Your Garden*. Today, gourds are also used for many purposes such as containers, birdhouses, musical instruments, and decoration. Coiling on gourds has been a technique used by many gourd artists. Natural and manmade materials are used including pine needles, kudzu, grasses, paper rush, cloth, wire, and many more. Basket weaving on gourds is basically a new technique, but any material used for baskets can be used to weave on gourds.

1.2: Cordage in the United States

Cordage was originally for making ropes and string, but functions well for weaving in baskets and for gourds. Ron Layton wrote an article in 2006 about cordage in North America. He gave me permission to reprint it here. Nancy Gildersleeve makes baskets and works on gourds. She uses many natural materials in her creations. She wrote a tutorial about making cordage and also gave permission for using it here.

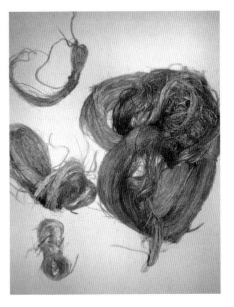

Dogbane fibers from Ron Layton. *Courtesy of Ron Layton.*

Cordage in North America
by Ron Layton © 2006

This article is about cordage, one of the most used and necessary items for day to day life. Other than sinew, catgut, and rawhide, early man made his rope and string from more readily available plant material. Certain plant fibers were able to stand up to water immersion and made excellent nets and fishing line. Animal fibers, such as sinew and catgut, would stretch or unravel when wet and were more difficult to procure. Plant fibers were so much more abundant and easier to process; this left sinew and catgut for sewing, bow backing, arrow making, and other arts requiring a strong, longer lasting material.

Another difference between plant and animal fibers is the strength comparison of a string made of sinew and a string of plant fiber. The plant fiber string, in most cases, would have to be twice the diameter of the sinew string to be of the same strength. Thus, for certain applications where weight and mass are important (such as arrow making) the thinner sinew would be the best choice. Sinew, catgut, and rawhide were not available in all areas since it usually comes from large animals. There aren't very many places in North America where a decent cordage fiber plant isn't available.

Cordage can be made from bark, branches, roots, stems, and leaves. In some rare cases the seed fluff from whorled milkweed and cottonwood was wound into cordage. This would be very labor intensive and was used mostly for ceremonial objects.

Trees can supply cordage by use of the bark, roots, and in a few cases, limbs. In the North, the roots of the spruce tree are used to make good, strong cordage. In the Great Lakes area, the Indians use this root for sewing the birch bark together on their canoes. The roots of the junipers, walnut, butternut, wild cherry, and Osage orange are used too. Roots that grow in fine or sandy soil are the most favored as they are usually straighter and have fewer deformities. They are split in two or more sections and sometimes the outer bark is rubbed off. This is accomplished by rubbing the root section back and forth over a limb with somewhat rough bark, as if you were sawing it. Some bark and root binding materials tend to get a little brittle as they dry, so they are often soaked in water for a while before use. From my experience, roots make the best bow drill string of all. Always try to take only a few roots from several different trees. This doesn't kill the tree and insures a future supply of roots.

The best bark cordage comes from small limbs. The bark is thinner, and this process won't harm the tree. The inner bark of juniper, elm, cottonwood, aspen, basswood, moosewood, maple, willow, and desert willow are the most often used. Basswood is one of the better sources of fine bark cordage. The limbs, and in the case of a freshly fallen tree, the trunk, are stripped of their

Dogbane cordage made by Ron Layton. *Courtesy of Ron Layton.*

bark. This bark is held submerged for a few weeks until the inner bark starts to come loose in layers. These strips are then dried and stored for future use. When some cordage is needed, they're soaked for a while before braiding or twisting. Slippery elm and willow bark make good, strong cordage. Most barks are best gathered May through August because the bark comes off a lot easier. Out of season, the bark can still be loosened and removed by pounding the limbs gently with a wood maul or mallet made from a branch about 3" in diameter. Another piece of thick branch should be used as an anvil. Both anvil and mallet should be made smooth as possible to deter ruining the bark. If you decide to use a rock for an anvil, the bark may be damaged beyond use. Pounding works well on such barks as pawpaw, hickory, elm, maple, willow, and poplar. I've used slippery elm with the outer bark removed, and it made very strong rope for a wickiup shelter I was building. Many shrubs such as sagebrush, cliffrose, and flannel bush have usable bark as well. As an aside, most of these barks are used in basketry too.

Most grass stems and leaves used for cordage, such as sweetgrass, dunegrass, and the reeds are used whole without much further processing. Cattail leaves when used whole are usually braided into a somewhat usable rope. When shredded lengthwise, they make stronger cordage after they've been twisted together. The leaves of agave, yucca, and iris must be processed in some way to get the fibers. Agave has a sharp point at the end of the leaf that is hard and dense. This "needle" can be carefully pulled downward towards the base of the leaf and several fibers will remain attached. This can be used as is for sewing. To get the most fibers from an agave leaf, it is usually gently pounded or "retted"—that is, soaked in water until the fleshy part of the leaf rots away. One should use caution when working with agave, as the fresh leaf contains chemicals that cause dermatitis.

I prefer working with yucca; it is a very versatile plant to work with. In Paul Campbell's book, *Survival Skills of Native California*, there are several photos and references to articles made from yucca cordage. It was used by Indian tribes throughout the West to make nets, bow strings, and many other items. You can use the leaves green or dry. I prefer to process the green leaves by retting. After I gather a good sized bunch, I put them in a five gallon bucket, fill it with water, and let it set for a few days. When I check them, I hope to find most of the fleshy material is rotted or beginning to rot (you can tell the retting process is working by the terrible smell!). If the leaves are really mushy, they have retted long enough to work the fibers free. I do this by laying the leaves a few at a time on a board and running an old wood rolling pin over them to squeeze out the plant material; then the leaf remains are swooshed around in a bucket of clean water and the fibers are fairly cleaned of plant material. I then wring the bundles of fiber out and give them another rinse. This loosens even more plant material and the shorter, unusable fibers. These hanks of fiber are hung up to dry and put away until I need to make some cordage. This is the easiest way I have found to process yucca. In the wilds you could do the same by putting them in a stream or pool and weighing them down.

If you use the dry yucca leaves, you will have to pound them with the mallet and anvil technique. The pounded

Cordage from Plants (North American)

by Ron Layton

Abutilon abutilon – Velvet Leaf, Indian Mallow (stem)

Acer glabrum – Rocky Mountain Maple (bark)

Acer macrophyllum – Bigleaf maple (bark)

Acorus calamus – Sweetflag (leaves)

Agave americana – American Century Plant (leaves)

Agave deserti – Desert Agave (leaves)

Agave lechuguilla – Lechuguilla (leaves)

Agave parryi – Parry Agave (leaves)

Agave schottii – Schott Agave (leaves)

Agave toumeyana – Toumey Agave (leaves)

Agave utahensis – Century Plant (leaves)

Althaea officinalis – Marsh Mallow (stem)

Amelanchier alnifolia – Saskatoon Serviceberry (branches)

Apocynum androsaemifolium – Dogbane (stem)

Apocynum cannabinum – Dogbane, Black Indian Hemp, Armyroot (stem)

Arctium lapa – Burdock (stem)

Argentina anserina – Silverweed Cinquefoil (runners)

Artemisia tridentata – Sagebrush (bark)

Asclepias asperula – Antelope Horns Milkweed (stem)

Asclepias erlocarpa – Woolypod Milkweed (stem)

Asclepias fascicularis – Mexican Whorled Milkweed (stem)

Asclepias hallii – Purple Milkweed (stem)

Asclepias incarnata – Swamp Milkweed (stem)

Asclepias lanceolata – Narrow Leaved Purple Milkweed (stem)

Asclepias ovalifolia – Milkweed (stem)

Asclepias pulchra – Hairy Milkweed, White Indian Hemp (stem)

Asclepias pumila – Low Milkweed (stem)

Asclepias purpurascens – Purple Milkweed (stem)

Asclepias quadrifolia – Fourleaf Milkweed (stem)

bundles are then rubbed between the hands to loosen any plant material. I've heard of some folks who use a dull knife or stone flake to scrape the leaves and expose the fibers. I have tried this, but with limited success. I once cooked some yucca leaves to see if this would make them easier to work, but found the resulting fibers were a bit too stiff and hash, unlike the smooth, soft fibers from the retting process. Iris leaves have only two usable fiber strands per leaf. The average iris leaf is only one or two feet long. These fibers were highly valued considering the amount of labor it took to get a usable amount. The leaves are split lengthwise with the thumbnail. Sometimes an artificial thumbnail is used. It is made from a mussel shell attached to the thumb with a bit of cordage. The two leaf halves are then scraped on both sides with the mussel shell thumbnail. This exposes a silky white fiber. The iris was mostly used in the Pacific Northwest and the fibers were twisted into cordage for fishing line, netting, snares, and many other items.

The stem sections of many different plants hold useful cordage fibers. Plants such as nettle, dogbane, velvet leaf, milkweed, prairie flax, thistle, and fireweed are valued for their quality fibers. I have processed many hundreds of feet of stinging nettle, dogbane, and milkweed cordage. These stems are hollow or have a pith core. They are collected in the fall after the last leaves have fallen off, usually after the first frost. The stems are left to dry in a warm place and then they are checked for brittleness. I then split them lengthwise, usually into four sections. These sections are easier to work with. Each section is carefully snapped every few inches, beginning at the bottom. As I snap each small section, I carefully peel the fiber bearing bark loose. Hopefully, I'll end up with a section of bark the full length of the stem. Short sections of bark are still useful as the fibers can be spliced onto longer sections of cordage. As I twist the sections into cordage, the dry, brittle bark falls off leaving nice silky fiber. Sometimes the cord has to be twisted back and forth several times to loosen stubborn bark fragments. Some folks use a knife to scrape the bark off the stem before sectioning it but I prefer to just let it fall off while twisting. If you're not careful, you can scrape too deep and ruin the fiber.

Vines and branches are used as cordage. Grapevine, greenbrier, and hazelnut are just a few of the many different plants used in this fashion. Most vines are used for lightweight tasks as they aren't very strong. Hazelnut withes are used to tie bundles of firewood, and a strong cord with tumpline is tied to the bundle for transportation. These withes can be bent double and are also used as handles on stone axes and hammers.

Several of the books in the bibliography illustrate the technique of turning fiber into cordage. Also, there are several sites on the Internet that illustrate the process of twisting fiber into cordage. If you are interested, do a Google® search for "cordage" and "primitive skills."

Bibliography:
Survival Skills of Native California, Paul Campbell;
Primitive Wilderness Living & Survival Skills Vol. 1 & 2, John & Geri McPherson;
Bushcraft, Mors Kochanski;
Any of the Peterson Field Guides on flowering plants, trees and shrubs; these guides are well illustrated and there are different guides for both the Eastern and Western United States.

Asclepias rubra – Red Milkweed (stem)
Asclepias speciosa – Showy Milkweed (stem)
Asclepias subverticillata – Whorled Milkweed (seed hair)
Asclepias syriaca – Common Milkweed (stem)
Asclepias tuberosa – Butterfly Weed, Pleurisy Root (stem)
Asclepias viridiflora – Green Milkweed (stem)
Asimina triloba – Pawpaw (bark & root)
Boehmeria cylindrica – False Nettle (stem)
Carex barbarae – Santa Barbara Sedge (root)
Carya – Hickory (bark & root)
Cedrus – Cedar (bark & root)
Cercis canadensis – California Redbud (bark)
Chamaecyparis nootkatensis – Alaska Cedar (bark)
Chamerion angustifolium – Fireweed (stem)
Chilopsis linearis – Desert Willow (bark)
Cirsium arvense – Canadian Thistle (stem)
Cirsium edule – Edible Thistle (stem)
Cirsium vulgare – Bull Thistle (stem)
Clematis ligusticifolia – Western White Clematis (stem)
Convolvulus arvensis – Field Bindweed (stem)
Cornus sericea – Redosier Dogwood (bark)
Corylus cornuta var. californica – California Hazelnut (twigs)
Corylus cornuta var. cornuta – Beaked Hazelnut (twigs)
Cowania mexicana – Cliffrose (bark)
Dirca palustris – Moosewood, Leatherwood (bark)
Elaeagnus commutata – Silverberry (bark)
Fraxinus – Ash (bark)
Fremontodendron californicum – California Flannelbush (bark)
Geranium atropurpureum – Western Purple Cranesbill (stem)

Glyceria canadensis – Sweetgrass (stem)
Gossypium hirsutum – Upland Cotton (fuzz)
Hoita macrostachya – Large Leatherroot (root)
Iris douglasiana – Western Iris (leaves)
Iris innominata – Del Norte County Iris (leaves & root)
Iris macrosiphon – Bowltube Iris (leaves)
Iris tenax – Klamath Iris (leaves)
Juglans cinerea – Butternut (bark)
Juglans nigra – Black Walnut (bark & root)
Juncus effusus – Common Rush (stem)
Juncus tenuis – Poverty Rush (stem)
Juniperus californica – California Juniper (bark & root)
Juniperus communis – Common Juniper (bark & root)
Juniperus deppiana – Alligator Juniper (bark & root)
Juniperus horizontalis – Creeping Juniper (bark & root)
Juniperus monosperma – Oneseed Juniper (bark & root)
Juniperus occidentalis – Western Juniper (bark & root)
Juniperus osteosperma – Utah Juniper (bark & root)
Laportea canadensis – Canadian Woodnettle (stem)
Larix laricina – Tamarack (root)
Leymus mollis – American Dunegrass (leaves)
Linaria linaria – Toad Flax (stem)
Linum lewisii – Prairie Flax (root & stem)
Liriodendron tulipifera – Tulip Tree (bark)
Lonicera ciliosa – Orange Honeysuckle (stem)
Lupinus arboreus – Bush Lupine (root)
Maclura pomifera – Osage Orange (root)
Morus alba – White Mulberry (root)
Morus microphylla – Texas Mulberry (root)
Morus rubra – Red Mulberry (root)
Nereocystis luetkeana – Bull Whip Kelp (stem)
Nolina microcarpa – Sacahuista (Agavaceae) (leaves)
Oenothera biennis – Evening Primrose (stem)
Phragmites communis – Reed Grass (stem & leaves)
Picea engelmannii – Engelmann's Spruce (root & limb)
Picea glauca – White Spruce (root)
Picea mariana – Black Spruce (root)
Picea sitchensis – Sitka Spruce (root)
Populus balsamifera – Brayshaw Black Cottonwood (bark)
Populus deltoides – Eastern Cottonwood (bark)
Populus fremontii – Fremont's Cottonwood (bark)
Populus tremuloides – Quaking Aspen (bark)
Potamogeton diversifolius – Waterthread Pondweed (stem)
Prosopis glandulosa – Honey Mesquite (bark)
Prunus emarginata – Bitter Cherry (bark & root)
Psoralea macrostachya – (stem)

Psoralidium lanceolatum – Lemon Scurfpea (root)
Quercus – Oak (bark & root)
Ribes divaricatum – Spreading Gooseberry (root)
Ribes lacustre – Prickly Currant (root)
Ribes lobbii – Gummy Gooseberry (root)
Robinia pseudoacacia – Black Locust (root)
Salix bebbiana – Beb Willow (bark)
Salix discolor – Pussy Willow (bark)
Salix exigua – Sandbar Willow (bark)
Salix laevigata – Red Willow (bark)
Salix lasiolepis – Arroyo Willow (bark)
Salix lucida – Pacific Willow (bark)
Salix lutea – Yellow Willow (bark)
Salix melanopsis – Dusky Willow (bark)
Salix scouleriana – Scouler's Willow (bark)
Salix sitchensis – Sitka Willow (bark)
Salvia – Sage (root)
Scirpus acutus – Beetle Hardstem Bulrush (root & stem)
Sesbania macrocarpa – Wild Hemp (stem)
Serenoa repens – Saw Palmetto (leaves)
Smilax – Greenbrier (vine)
Taxodium distichum – Baldcypress (bark)
Thuja plicata – Western Redcedar (bark & limbs)
Tilia americana – Basswood (bark)
Tillandsia usneoides – Spanish Moss (stem)
Tsuga canadensis – Eastern Hemlock(root)
Typha latifolia – Broad-leaved Cattail (leaves)
Typha angustifolia – Narrow-leaved Cattail (leaves)
Typha domingensis – Southern Cattail (leaves)
Ulmus rubra – Slippery Elm (bark & root)
Urtica dioica – Stinging Nettle (stem)
Urtica dioica ssp. holosericea – Stinging Nettle (stem)
Urtica dioica ssp. gracilis – California Nettle (stem)
Vicia americana – American Vetch (root)
Vitis aestivalis – Summer Grape (vine)
Vitis californica – California Wild Grape (vine)
Yucca angustissima – Narrowleaf Yucca (leaves)
Yucca baccata – Banana Yucca (leaves)
Yucca baileyi – Navajo Yucca (leaves)
Yucca brevifolia – Joshua Tree (leaves)
Yucca elata – Soaptree Yucca (leaves)
Yucca glauca – Small Soapweed (leaves)
Yucca harrimaniae – Spanish Bayonet (leaves)
Yucca shidigera – Mojave Yucca (leaves)
Yucca schottii – Schott Yucca (leaves)
Yucca whipplei – Chaparral Yucca (leaves)

Making Cordage
by Nancy Gildersleeve

Cordage (rope) has been made since the earliest of days when it was needed to lash all sorts of things together, from shelter supports to burden bundles. Examples of Calusa fishing nets dating from 700-1500 AD made of palm fiber cordage are on display at the Florida Museum of Natural History (Gainesville), along with an excellent video of cordage making. In the South, the husks from field corn have been twisted into rope and used for chair seats for many years. Cattails are another seating material, used for cordage in other places. Hong Kong grass is a Far East cordage material used today as basket rim fillers and for seats.

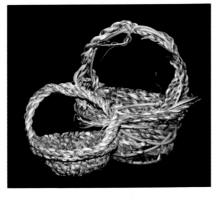

Nancy Gildersleeve made this basket using daylily cordage and peeled honeysuckle sewn with artificial sinew. *Photography by Kelly Hazel.*

Cordage from yucca, daylily, papyrus. *Courtesy of Nancy Gildersleeve. Photography by Kelly Hazel.*

Plants with long strong leaves work well for cordage. Daylily, iris, and border grass varieties are good. Pull or cut the leaves at the end of the growing season but before they freeze or start to crumble. Bundle them in small clumps and hang to dry. Experiment with plants available to you, some will be too soft to make a strong cord but might work combined with another plant.

One of the best cordage fibers comes from *yucca filamentosa* (bear grass), a Florida native that grows in rosettes of long (two to three foot) strong leaves. These can be split into fibers. Another yucca, *yucca aloifolia* (Spanish bayonet) is a common landscape plant with thick leaves, which must be pounded to release the fibers. Cordage has been made from Spanish moss and from many roots and barks, especially mulberry, cedar, and cypress. The Calusa nets were made from the thin strings found on Sabal palmetto fronds.

Cordage making is similar to spinning, except that the fibers are twisted and plied together at the same time. One method involves rolling the fibers down the thigh, another both hands with the fibers hooked over a peg, nail, or tree branch. The two hand method used one hand to do the twisting, the other to hold the completed cord and keep the twist from unraveling.

To prepare dried plant material for cordage, soak it in hot water for ten minutes or less. Dip a terrycloth towel in hot water and wring it out. Wrap the soaked plant material in the towel and let it sit for a few minutes to mellow. Find a shallow bowl or cup of water to keep your fingers moist. When you are ready to begin, take two leaves from the towel and tie their butt ends together. You may also split a single broad leaf along the center rib toward the butt end and keep that end intact.

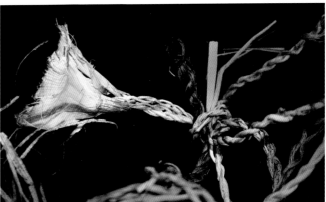

Yucca filamentosa is a native Florida plant. *Courtesy of Nancy Gildersleeve.*

Nancy Gildersleeve splitting the yucca to use for cordage. *Courtesy of Nancy Gildersleeve.*

1.3: Traditional Weaving Materials

Coils of commercially purchased reed. *Photography by Kelly Hazel.*

Rattan

There are about 600 species of rattan. They are native to Indochina, the Philippines, and the Pacific. It is a tropical plant that climbs through the rain forest. Rattan for commercial use is harvested mostly in the jungles of southeast Asia and Indonesia. It has a thorny bark that can be stripped away to reveal a tough, shiny layer, which is called cane. The cane is split and can be used for weaving baskets. This is what the Nantucket basket makers use to weave their baskets. Reed, the most commonly used material for baskets today, is the inner pith or core of the rattan plant. It is cut and smoothed into different sizes of reed to be used for weaving and in making furniture. It is flexible and sturdy and porous, so it can take stain and dyes easily. There are many weaving suppliers of cane and reed. An extensive list is included in this book.

Diamonds All Around by Pati English. The Cherokee diamond design is a continuous diamond pattern between the mountain peaks or arrows. Without a pattern break, the basket is woven in reed, dyed in the artist's studio with natural walnuts and scarlet red fabric dye. *Photography by Kelly Hazel.*

White Oak

White oak was the primary material used by the central and southern Appalachian Mountain regions. It was also used by the Cherokee in the southeast. There are two species in the white oak group. The common white oak, Quercus alba, was used by the Appalachian weavers. The other species, the swamp chestnut oak or Quercus michauxii, was used mainly in the deep south. White oak is abundant, but not all trees are suitable for making basket splints. The best trees are found in the rich bottomlands where they are protected from the weather. The best tree is small and approximately four to eight inches at the base. It is usually a tree that is twenty to thirty years old. It must be tall and straight with no marks or blemishes for about four to six feet from the base of the tree. White oak should be cut when green and wet with sap. It can be cut in the fall and winter, because it will stay green for up to six months. The tree is split from the top end and working to the bottom. It is split in halves, then into quarters, and then in eighths. From the eighths, the wood is split in line with the growth rings. A heavy knife is used to start the split. The knife-started-splits are then carefully pulled apart by hand. The hand splits are smoothed and scraped to the desired width. Berea College Appalachian Museum published a catalog entitled *Ribs, Rods, and Splits*. This catalog has some very good information about preparing white oak. Much of their information came from the book, *Appalachian White Oak Basketmaking: Handing Down the Tradition*, by Cynthia Taylor and Rachel Nash Law.

White oak basket, woven by the author. *Photography by Kelly Hazel.*

White oak basket in author's collection. Artist unknown. *Photography by Kelly Hazel.*

An unknown artist created this Cherokee basket woven with white oak that is in the author's collection. *Photography by Kelly Hazel.*

The Cherokee also use white oak, Quercus alba, as a weaving material. It is a forest hard wood. They look for a ten to twelve year old sapling about six inches in diameter that is straight and tall with few branches. Once the tree is cut, there are several other procedures that must be done before the oak can be used for weaving, such as quartering, splitting, trimming, and dyeing. Many years ago, I went with a group into a forest in search of a proper white oak. We searched for a long time before finding a small tree. We cut the tree and then cut the log into sections. We took the tree back to a barn to split and sand the wood into splints for weaving. It was a very hard job, so I now order my oak from suppliers.

Black ash basket made by the author.
Photography by Kelly Hazel.

Ash

There are several species of ash: black, white, and brown. Black ash, Fraxinus nigra, is a swamp tree and grows throughout the northeastern United States and southern Canada. It grows in swamps and along lakes, rivers, and streams. In northern New England, it is called brown ash. It is arguable that this tree is different than the black ash as it likes its feet wet, but needs full sun. It is a ring porous tree that is pounded into ring splints. Black ash has also been called brown ash, hoop ash, swamp ash, water ash, and basket ash. The best time to cut the tree is in the spring when the sap is rising. If it is cut in the winter or fall, it must be submerged in water to keep it moist. It will be good to use for up to six months. White ash, Fraxinus latifolia, grows in abundance in Oregon. Only about six feet of the tree trunk will be used for making basket supplies. When the Native Americans cut an ash tree, they would cut up what would not be used into small pieces so it could go back into the ground to replenish the earth. This practice is still used today. The tree would be stripped of the outer bark. The log would be soaked about a week before harvesting the splints.

For the black and white ash, the log is pounded with a wooden mallet to loosen the growth rings. Pound until the log is about four inches in diameter. Each growth ring has a porous area that is open between it and the next year's growth. Bundle the splints and use the heavy log left for handles. When you are ready to weave, soak the splints in warm water and separate them in half. Then you can cut the sizes you need. Black ash does not have a bad side. The white ash is scraped on the rough side. The pieces can be split by hand for thinner pieces. When weaving with ash, you will need to keep it damp. Do not keep it too wet as it will swell and when the basket dries, it will shrink. Pack the rows as you weave. You can also weave part of the basket and then let it dry so you can pack, then dampen, and finish and pack again at the end. Before adding the rim, be sure all rows are packed tightly. Susi Nuss has some wonderful information on preparing ash on her web site, www.BasketMakers.org. Harvesting ash is a very hard job, just like the white oak. There are suppliers who sell beautiful ash splints for weaving. Again, check the suppliers list in this book.

Ash basket made by author.
Photography by Kelly Hazel.

1.4: Vines

There are many kinds of vines growing all over the world. Many of these vines have been used by different cultures to create baskets. A vine, according to Wikipedia, the free online encyclopedia, is "any climbing or trailing plant." The best time of the year to collect vines will be in the winter. For woody vines, like honeysuckle, Virginia creeper, wisteria, and grapevine, it is better to collect them before the sap begins to rise. It is also easier as there are fewer leaves to deal with. Try to collect ones that are flexible for weaving. For spokes, thicker vines can be used. Some vines need to be collected green. Nancy Basket collects kudzu vines green. In the following, you will find some information about collecting kudzu and other types of vines and how to prepare them for weaving. Just remember, wherever you collect your vines or any natural material, get permission from the owner of the land. If it is government or federal land, make sure you check the regulations for gathering materials from that area.

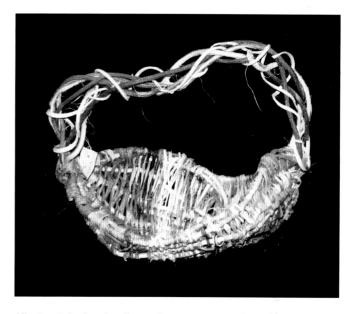

All wisteria basket, handle was from a segment where three vines had grown together. Spokes were used unpeeled, weavers were split. Basket is about 25" each dimension. Made by Nancy Gildersleeve. *Photography by Kelly Hazel.*

Kudzu

Kudzu is a climbing, coiling, and trailing vine that is native to southern Japan and southeast China. Kudzu was first introduced in the United States at the 1876 Centennial Exposition in Philadelphia, Pennsylvania. At this 100th birthday of the United States, the Japanese government displayed a beautiful garden full of ornamental plants. One of these was kudzu. Some American garden suppliers sold kudzu plants by mail after the exposition. During the 1930s Great Depression, the Soil Conservation Service promoted kudzu for erosion control. In the 1940s, farmers were paid to plant kudzu. The problem with kudzu in the southern part of the United States is that there are no natural insect enemies of the vine and the long, warm growing seasons promote the growth of the vine. So it grows out-of-control in many places. In China and Japan, kudzu is used for food and even medicine. In the United States, crafters have found uses by making kudzu furniture, baskets, and other items.

Kudzu vines and leaves at Nancy Basket's house. *Photography by Kelly Hazel.*

Nancy Basket splitting kudzu vine in front of the kudzu bale barn. *Photography by Kelly Hazel.*

Nancy Basket, who lives in Walhalla, South Carolina, has been making kudzu baskets for a long time. Her Cherokee heritage has inspired many of her creations. Nancy says, "An old saying goes, 'If you're going to plant kudzu, drop it and run.' The vine grows up to a foot a day during summer months and chokes the southeastern landscape with a dense, green mat of foliage." Folklore is often the inspiration for her weavings and the kudzu paper she makes is turned into beautiful cards and pictures. Nancy's website, www. Nancybasket.com, offers various items made from kudzu vine such as jelly, candy, paper, and others.

Nancy shared with me how to collect and prepare kudzu for making baskets. Since kudzu is so prolific in the South, maybe you can try weaving a kudzu basket. Nancy even constructed a barn out of kudzu bales. The following information about kudzu is from Nancy Basket.

Collecting Kudzu

Kudzu blossoms bloom in late summer, and they smell like grape bubble gum. They grow up on long spikes from the bottom first, then middle, and finally the tops. They grow under the shade of the large leaves so they last longer in hot southern summers. Leaves on the kudzu have small hairs on them that may irritate some people when they pull them off the vines. Kudzu is not like poison ivy, the larger the vine, the fewer the leaves. You may want to wear long sleeves when gathering the vines.

Since kudzu grows twelve inches a day, you can collect it all year long. The younger vines die back at first frost, but the older growth, dormant in winter, is green all year. Always cut kudzu green, when the inside is white. Choose the vines growing up into trees that are about as thick as your thumb. Avoid the curled ones as they are harder to split. Larger vines are more fibrous. Smaller vines snap like green beans, as kudzu is a legume, and the pithy white inside has not yet developed the fiber that it will when it ages.

It is best to stay at the side of smaller roads to collect kudzu. In the South, kudzu covers many sides of freeways. According to Nancy, "Stopping there to collect basketry or gourd materials does not constitute an emergency and could cost you upwards of $200, as a friend of mine found out once. Going into the middle of a patch is not necessarily 'snaky', but kudzu may cover up open wells, barbed wire or rusty tin. Look for poison ivy and anthills before you start cutting. If they are there, go somewhere else! In more than twenty years being in the fields, the following saying has worked for me and I never see snakes: 'Brother and Sister Snake, I'm coming through. Watch out for me as I'm watching out for you and Poison Ivy, Creepy Crawlies that means you, too'!"

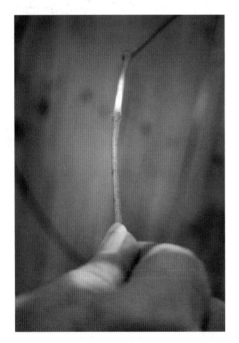

Small kudzu vine. *Photography by Kelly Hazel.*

Remember, vines that grow up in the tree are good ones to look for. Cut the vine as low to the ground as you can and as high as you can. Avoid pulling on the vine too much as it could be holding up a heavy, dead tree limb. Depending on the diameter of the vine, kudzu will last several days before you split it. After that, it turns hard and brown; soaking it does little good. Sap runs in the plant in the spring and summer. The outside bark will always come off and can be used for color contrasts. The vine may drip a clear, watery fluid that sometimes stains. It can be consumed if you are not allergic, which few people are. In the fall and winter, the plant is lighter in weight and is still easy to split but the bark remains on.

Preparing Kudzu

Cut the vines into three foot sections. Larger, ground-running vines can be cut as well. Kudzu vines have interesting roots that can be washed and woven into organic looking baskets. Nancy said that "stories are told that baskets made fresh this way, in Florida, will begin to grow from these roots when hung up. For more than twenty years, this has never happened to me. Kudzu does not have the properties of wood like locust, where fence posts have been made and later have started sprouting! Once a southern seed company sold kudzu seeds as 'Jack in the Bean Stalk Vines', but they no longer do this." Please consult your state to find out if kudzu is considered an invasive plant.

Above from left:
Nancy Basket pulling kudzu vine from the tree to get as much length as possible. *Photography by Kelly Hazel.*

Nancy Basket cutting kudzu vine. *Photography by Kelly Hazel.*

Nancy Basket cuts the kudzu vines when they are thumb size or thicker. *Photography by Kelly Hazel.*

To split kudzu, cut a cross into the end of a vine so that you can grab each half at the same time. Pull on both sides equally all the way to the end. It will sound like a zipper and smell like fresh green apples or maybe pumpkin. When the kudzu splits unevenly, pull on the thicker side, only to get it centered again. The thin, short pieces you will get at first, because you're not experienced, make excellent material for attaching to gourds. More mature kudzu has a small, white, pithy core. It is not fungus, as some may think, and does not have to be cut off. It has a foam core feel. Keep splitting the vine until you have the desired thinness. It is supple enough to tie knots in the end of the pieces. Threadlike is too small for random freeform coiling, but makes great miniatures.

Kudzu shrinks as it dries, so later on your basket could be too loose. You can let it dry, then moisten it a little before working with it. You can do this by wrapping the kudzu in a damp towel for a few minutes. Do not put moist kudzu in plastic as it will turn brown and mold. Split kudzu can be coiled into a circle, dried, and worked with later. Use the dark bark as well as the white vine for natural color. Reconstituted vines are more yellow in color. Kudzu can be braided or corded into strong rope. You don't have to split the vine, but it can be used whole to weave with. Drying kudzu for a few days after harvesting will allow some shrinkage.

Nancy Basket in front of kudzu bale barn cutting kudzu vine into sections before splitting it. *Photography by Kelly Hazel.*

Nancy Basket splitting kudzu vine down the center pith (styrofoam-like center). *Photography by Kelly Hazel.*

Nancy Basket is pulling kudzu bark away from the stem. It pulls away easily in the summer. *Photography by Kelly Hazel.*

Nancy Basket is pulling the kudzu vine into pieces. *Photography by Kelly Hazel.*

Nancy Basket continues to pull the vine into pieces to get the fibers. *Photography by Kelly Hazel.*

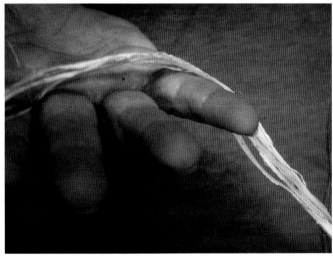

Inner bark of kudzu used for making weavings or cloth. *Courtesy of Nancy Basket. Photography by Kelly Hazel.*

Dyeing Kudzu

Indigo dye works on kudzu in the first dipping. Other dyes work well, too. Split the vine as thin as you want it to be before you dye it because only the outside takes the dye. Splitting the kudzu after dying it gives you a variegated look. Soak the colored vines in vinegar to set the dye. The outer bark dyes darker than the whiter parts

Uses for Kudzu

Split Kudzu Uses

According to Nancy Basket, "Fibrous ceilings can be made from split kudzu. Using steel grids, I wove kudzu in a pattern through four inch openings for a 600 foot long entrance into a restaurant in Las Vegas one summer. The finished piece looked like an overhead river. Room dividers can be made by attaching two or three old screen doors together. Remove rusty screens and use thin kudzu to weave in the opening. Large lamps can be made by making a frame and weaving over that. Kudzu curtains can be woven for windows or wall hangings can be made on large frames. Old chairs with no seats can sport new rears by using kudzu, split or not."

Author made this small kudzu basket at a workshop with Nancy Basket. *Photography by Kelly Hazel.*

Kudzu Inner Bark Uses

In spring, the outer bark on kudzu peels away in a very thin layer. Sometimes the green stays on the inner bark for another natural color in your basket. In winter, the inner bark is harder to separate. Inner bark can be quickly torn apart in long lengths when it is fresh off the vine. It can be dried for later use in weaving projects. These very thin fibers are great for coiling on gourds. Clothing can also be made from the inner bark. The easiest way to do this is to get green vines thinner than your pinky finger and put them in your compost pile for a few days. They will need cleaning! Hose them down and if fermented long enough, the thin inner bark will come away easily from the white foam core looking center and outer bark. These fibers will be thin, translucent, and ready to weave. Tie them together end to end and wind them on a bobbin. The warp and weft of your weaving project can be made from kudzu or the warp can be a cotton thread. You may want to see how the fiber works by working on a book cover first.

Detail of inner kudzu bark weaving on a loom. *Courtesy of Nancy Basket. Photography by Kelly Hazel.*

Green Vine Preparation for Weaving

Young green vines can be gathered as long as possible, coiled into a pot and boiled for a couple of hours. Hose them off and scrape the green goo with a small paint scraper to get thin strips. The inside white pith looks like long caterpillars. Wash the fibers well and they can be used as the weft in weaving. Finer outer bark fibers can be gathered from this mess and used in more detailed projects. This type of fiber is thicker and flatter compared to the fermentation method. Remember to tell people what materials you use when selling your baskets. Also, tell them how long the process takes.

Paper Coils From Kudzu

Paper coils that some weavers use on gourds and in baskets are machine processed. You can make your own coils. The Japanese art of "shifu" is intricate, time consuming, and takes a great deal of practice, but cloth can be made this way. Rougher coils for baskets or gourds are possible until you learn how to cut the paper into very thin strips, roll them, wet them, and spin into a "yarn." You can also make paper from kudzu leaves with the recipe on Nancy Basket's website (www.nancybasket.com).

If you decide to make paper from kudzu, remember that leaves from this vine have fibers that are extremely strong, unless they are chopped into one inch pieces or retted (soaking to wet the fibers so that bacterial action can facilitate separation of the fibers from the woody stem). They can wrap around the blades of your blender and choke it to death, so use blenders with strong motors. Information on this technique and how to use this method of cutting the folded paper into much wider widths can be found online. Check the list of resources for web sites. Try and experiment to see what you can do with a few sheets of paper. Rough rolls would work on gourds.

Oak basket with split kudzu inner fiber used for weavings. *Courtesy of Nancy Basket. Photography by Kelly Hazel.*

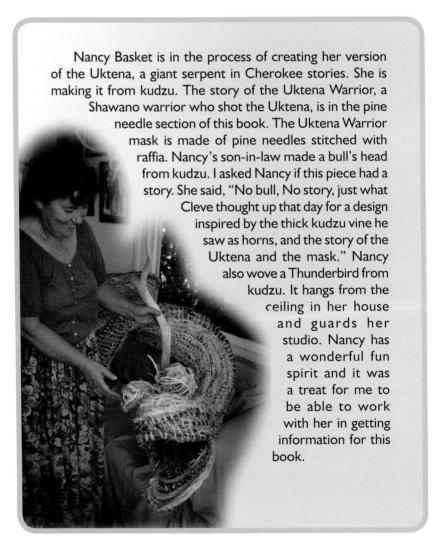

Nancy Basket is in the process of creating her version of the Uktena, a giant serpent in Cherokee stories. She is making it from kudzu. The story of the Uktena Warrior, a Shawano warrior who shot the Uktena, is in the pine needle section of this book. The Uktena Warrior mask is made of pine needles stitched with raffia. Nancy's son-in-law made a bull's head from kudzu. I asked Nancy if this piece had a story. She said, "No bull, No story, just what Cleve thought up that day for a design inspired by the thick kudzu vine he saw as horns, and the story of the Uktena and the mask." Nancy also wove a Thunderbird from kudzu. It hangs from the ceiling in her house and guards her studio. Nancy has a wonderful fun spirit and it was a treat for me to be able to work with her in getting information for this book.

Close up of the weaving in the Uktena's body. It is woven with kudzu bark and stitched with raffia. *Courtesy of Nancy Basket. Photography by Kelly Hazel.*

Close up of Thunderbird's head. *Courtesy of Nancy Basket. Photography by Kelly Hazel.*

Nancy Basket made the Thunderbird using kudzu bark and stitched with raffia. It hangs from the ceiling in her house. *Courtesy of Nancy Basket. Photography by Kelly Hazel.*

Close up of Cleve's bull. *Courtesy of Nancy Basket. Photography by Kelly Hazel.*

Cleve Phillips is Nancy Basket's son-in-law. He made the bull's head with kudzu bark stitched with raffia. The horns are thick kudzu vines. *Courtesy of Nancy Basket. Photography by Kelly Hazel.*

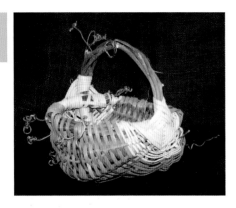

Karen Hafer used wild grapevine as the frame for this ribbed basket. *Courtesy of Karen Hafer.*

Close up of wild grapefruit vine. The ribs and frame are wild grapevine and it is woven with reed. *Courtesy of Karen Hafer.*

Young grapevine leaves in Nancy Basket's yard. *Photography by Kelly Hazel.*

Grapevines

Harvesting Wild Grapevines

Karen Hafer is a gourd artist and basket maker in White Hall, Maryland. She gathers some of her own natural materials, wild grapevine being one of them. The following is information she gave me for gathering and preparing wild grapevine.

"The wild grapevines are plentiful on our property, and are fun to harvest for weaving projects or wreaths. To gather them, choose living vines, which will be the most pliable, and use pruning shears to clip them close to the base. Pull the vines from the trees, keeping the pieces as long as possible. (Don't pull down any hairy-looking vines—those are the dreaded poison ivy!) Prune the unsightly or crooked parts off, but leave the curly tendrils. Either harvest when the vines are leafless, or remove the leaves as you cut the vines. Lay the lengths out on the ground in a straight line. In order to transport them, it is practical to form them into wreath shapes at the site and they can be kept on hand in a tidy manner. To do this, grasp the two ends of a piece of vine and form a circle of approximately 15" in diameter in the center of the length. Start wrapping it around itself as if you were making a wreath and twist the ends of the vine (one at a time) around and in and out, going in the same direction, to hold the circular shape. When you are ready to utilize the vine in a project, simply take the wreath apart by unwinding the vine. The sooner you use the vines, the more pliable they will be. Soaking them in a tub of warm water will make older vines more pliable. The loose bark may either be stripped off or left on for a more rustic look."

The following is some more information about grapevines that Nancy Basket shared with me. "Grapevines can be gathered all year, but do not split them. Use clippers to cut the small vines and loppers when they are bigger in diameter. When young, their tendrils add texture. This material can be coiled when smaller for use on gourd tops and used in random free form styles. When the vines are thicker, use the older fresh ones to either weave or randomly freeform into large baskets. Instead of tying knots into the ends and continuing, back the end piece around another vine to hold in place. Be careful of building baskets outside as they look smaller than they are and sometimes they don't fit in doorways when you bring them in!"

Muscadine Vines

Muscadine vines grow all over the southern part of the United States. This vine climbs high and has shredding bark and forked tendrils. Muscadine grows wild and also has been cultivated for use in wine making. You can gather the vines any time of the year. Select the longest vines for cutting. Trim off all leaves and then boil in water for one hour. Strip off the bark and then you can split the vine to the desired width. Wrap in paper bags and store in a dry, cool place. Soak for about twenty to thirty minutes before using.

Wisteria

I live in Greenville, South Carolina, and wisteria is abundant. I collect the thick, older vines and immediately coil them into circles, as I will use them to make frames for wisteria rib baskets. You can also use the thicker vines for spokes and the smaller vines for weaving in the basket. Wisteria does not shrink as much as kudzu, so the basket frame does not need to dry as long as a kudzu frame. I still pack the materials as I weave in order to make sure there are no large gaps in the finished basket.

Nancy Basket had this to say about wisteria. "Wisteria can be split, but it is harder to do than kudzu. I prefer splitting vines and coiling rather than weaving, as the material goes farther and is more unusual. Spring and summer seem to be the best times to gather this material, when the sap flows. The ground runners tend to break off in short pieces when trying to split them. The vine is more yellow in color, less fibrous, and splits flatter, more like reed. Many basket weavers prefer no hairs and like the wood neat and trimmed. We wild women prefer the nature of the vines to remain unshorn. Recognize the difference in vines growing close to you by observing them seasonally. Flowers from this vine bloom in spring and hang down from the tree in grape-like clusters, but smell like perfume. Smaller vines need not be split. They are very woody and shrink minimally."

Honeysuckle

The following information about honeysuckle came from Nancy Basket: "There are about twenty native species of honeysuckle in North America. This plant is best gathered where it grows long and straight, usually beside a creek. It cannot be split. When it winds over fences or itself, joints will form and it breaks easily. Leave the bark on to allow beautiful shades of brown in your basket. The bark can be boiled off in winter to get a white core underneath. As it gets older, the larger vines are white and flaky. Cherokee use honeysuckle woven over stronger oak splints in one type of traditionally woven basket. Almost any type of small vine can be coiled in baskets and used on gourds."

Honeysuckle vines make very nice smaller baskets. In fact, a lot of miniature baskets are woven with small honeysuckle vines. The Cherokee, who make beautiful honeysuckle baskets, even used sand to polish the vines before weaving in order to make them smoother. When I gather honeysuckle vines, I cut some large vines for spokes and some smaller vines for the weavers. The longer runners are the best for using as weavers. It can be gathered any time of the year, but the best time is after the sap is down. Make sure the vines are one or two years old if you want to use them for weavers. The larger, older vines can be used for rims, handles, and spokes in rib baskets. Cut the vine off near the root and strip off the leaves and branches. Coil the vines and submerge in water to boil. Boil for three to four hours. You can let the vines sit in the water overnight after boiling. Remove the bark and hang to dry. Coil in bundles until you are ready to use them. Before weaving, soak in water about for ten minutes.

Wisteria vine is coiled after harvesting. Large pieces can be used for the frame and ribs for a rib basket. Smaller pieces can be used for weavers. *Photography by Kelly Hazel.*

Close up of wisteria vines. *Photography by Kelly Hazel.*

Honeysuckle vine. *Courtesy of Nancy Basket. Photography by Kelly Hazel.*

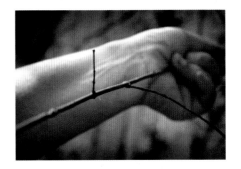

Fresh vines are good for free formed baskets. *Courtesy of Nancy Basket. Photography by Kelly Hazel.*

Large honeysuckle vine that was boiled for four hours and the bark stripped. It has a rust color. *Photography by Kelly Hazel.*

Small Cherokee honeysuckle vine basket in author's collection. Artist unknown. *Photography by Kelly Hazel.*

Small honeysuckle rib basket made by the author. Bark is used to make God's eye to hold frame together. *Photography by Kelly Hazel.*

Yellow jasmine vine. *Courtesy of Nancy Basket. Photography by Kelly Hazel.*

Yellow Jasmine

Nancy Basket says, "This thin vine is small and grows abundantly up and over trees in the South. It is South Carolina's state flower. Clip this woody vine that darkens to deep browns any time of year. It grows quickly and needs pruning anyway. Use it then or coil it and let it dry. Rehydrate to use. Warm water hastens pliability. This vine is good for random freeform designs or for shaping them into quick nests or used for coiling."

My neighbor has yellow jasmine growing up the side of her house. In the spring, the small yellow flowers are beautiful. In the winter, the small vines are long and rambling. Yellow Jasmine is not heavy enough to make a framework, but for weaving into a basket or weaving on top of a gourd, it is perfect. I use the vine naturally without scraping the skin off.

Virginia Creeper

Again, Nancy Basket gave me information on Virginia creeper. "This fast growing trailing vine has five leaves and is mistaken for poison ivy at times. It also has sucker feet that attach to trees or buildings, great for unique textures. The woody stem has small hairs on it as it gets bigger. Used fresh it would make an unusual gourd border. In states with high humidity the hairs would probably stay intact."

Marla Helton collects and uses Virginia creeper and gave me the following information. "Virginia creeper looks very similar to poison ivy so it is very important to check out some books to make sure you aren't harvesting poison ivy! You can usually harvest the vine from late spring until fall, depending on how thick you want the vine to be. Take clippers and clip one piece and drag it off the tree. The vines can be quite long, so sometimes it is necessary to cut them before they actually come off the tree. Cut off the long lateral vines and put those into a pile. Then, coil the vines and set them out to cure for a few days. The vines are still flexible enough to use in weaving. It is important to keep in mind that the vines will shrink considerably, so they must be woven either with another fiber or must be woven extremely tight if you want a solid look to the weaving. The vines can be woven loosely or braided, depending on the look you want."

Virginia creeper vine. *Courtesy of Nancy Basket. Photography by Kelly Hazel.*

Other Vines

There are other vines suitable for weaving or coiling. You will collect and prepare them in the same way as the vines above. Some other vines that can be used are trumpet vine, clematis, English ivy, Boston ivy, bittersweet, morning glory, silver lace, and others. Bittersweet can be found in mountain areas. They like dense growth and will twist and twine around trees. In autumn, the leaves turn a bright orange and yellow. The American bittersweet has yellow berries that grow at the tips of the branches. The fibrous core of the vine is very strong and makes a sturdy weaving material. The smaller vines are good for weaving and the larger ones are good for the framework in rib baskets and the twisted ones make wonderful handles. American bittersweet is found naturally in the central and eastern United States. Rehydrate, except in Florida. One word of caution: many of these vines are very invasive, like silver lace and honeysuckle, and can take over a landscape. Planting them in your back yard could cause a problem, especially if you have a small yard. Some of the vines have beautiful flowers that attract hummingbirds and bees. Many of the vines can be found in the forest, fields, and along the roadside. Be sure to get permission to collect vines that are not on your property. Some of these vines may even be in your neighbor's yard. They may be delighted for you to come and take all you want. In fact, I had a neighbor who said she would pay me to take her wisteria vines. Gugo vine is a naturally curvy vine, sometimes used in the workmanship of the basket and often as handles. Gugo vines grow in the mountains of the Philippines. Many vines can be ordered through suppliers or sometimes found at floral shops, and make wonderful framework or weaving material for rib baskets.

Flowers on the trumpet vine. *Courtesy of Nancy Basket. Photography by Kelly Hazel.*

Trumpet vine pods. *Courtesy of Nancy Basket. Photography by Kelly Hazel.*

English Ivy growing in author's neighbor's front yard. *Photography by Kelly Hazel.*

Close up of English ivy. *Photography by Kelly Hazel.*

1.5: Plants

There are many plants that can be used for weaving and coiling, such as iris, daylily, cattails, rushes, river cane, philodendron, horsetail, lavender, and many others. Many weavers experiment with various plants to see if they are suitable for weaving or coiling. You can use many of these plants for making cordage. The cordage can then be woven in baskets or coiled on gourds. Later in the book you will learn about making cordage.

Iris and Daylily

Gloria Christian, who lives in Alabama, uses iris leaves when she coils on gourds. In mid- and late summer through early fall, she pulls the bottom leaves off when they die. Before coiling, she soaks them in warm water for about five minutes to soften and rinses, removing dirt and pollen. She soaks them again in warm water and a tablespoon of glycerin for another five minutes and stirs often. This ensures that all the leaves are moistened. Before using, pat the leaves dry so they do not drip when working with them. Gloria wrote a tutorial on coiling with iris leaves on a gourd. You can find it in the project section. Marla Helton also uses daylily leaves in some of her baskets.

There are many species of iris. Bearded iris has dense hair lines along the midrib of the lower petals. They have sword-shaped leaves. The beardless iris has a long, narrow flower and is grown in home gardens, pond regions, marshes, and meadows. They are good for coiling materials. Harvest them in the late summer and early fall. Many natural weavers use Siberian iris leaves for coiling and weaving. The stems can be used for the core in the coiling. I have iris and daylily growing in my yard. In the fall, the leaves turn a golden color. They should be cut at the base and then rinsed off. Soak them in water for about five or ten minutes, then string them and hang to dry. When they are completely dry, put them in paper bags to store. Before weaving, soak them in warm water. You can mellow them by putting them in a damp towel. The leaves can be bundled and used for the core in coiling, or they can be used for weaving. If you want a stronger basket, use a stronger material for the base and weave in the leaves. I use the leaves in the natural weaving I do on top of gourds by using reed for the spokes and then softer materials can be woven in the gourd basket. Experiment and try using these leaves in your weaving.

From top:
Gloria Christian uses iris leaves to coil on a gourd. Here she also added a dried magnolia flower as an embellishment. *Courtesy of Gloria Christian.*

Marla Helton made this basket using reed, coir, and daylily leaves. It is titled *Sweet Annie. Photography by Stuart A. Fabe.*

New iris leaves growing from rhizomes. These are in the author's front yard. *Photography by Kelly Hazel.*

Dandelion

Pamela Zimmerman, who lives in North Carolina, uses a variety of natural materials in her more contemporary weavings. In the piece titled, Uprooted, she used dandelion stems. This is how she harvests and uses them: "I pick only monster dandelions. I like ones a foot tall or taller, and with stems as big around as my little finger, if I can find them. The flower grows taller when it goes into seed, so harvesting later is better. It is best when the seeds are flying. To collect, run your hand down the stem to the very bottom. There are 2-4 or more inches laying along the ground that you will not get if you do not reach for it. This is a little dangerous, given where monster dandelions grow—watch for fire ants, glass, etc. Leave the little flower head platforms ON but remove all the seeds. If you do not remove the seeds from inside a closed seedpod, it will open in your drying space and dust you with seeds. Make bundles as big as you can reach around with one hand. Bind the top just under the collected seed heads with a rubber band. Hang from the ceiling to dry. They will shrink enormously, but hanging them by the seed heads will allow them to continue hanging, as the heads are significantly larger than the stems. When dry, they will be like little dried up worms, and a totally different color. Watch carefully for mildew, they are very moist and must be hung in a dry area. I did not have good luck with the garage; it works better inside my studio. To use, dunk quickly in hot water, and mellow in a towel. Use for twining or coiling. This is a very fragile material."

Uprooted by Pamela Zimmerman is woven with dandelion stems, processed yucca fiber, hardwood tree roots with dirt, palm inflorescence, waxed linen, round reed, and copper. *Photography by Ronald L. Sowers Photography.*

Cattails

Cattails are a perennial plant. The cattail grows like iris and daylily flowers from rhizomes. They grow in marshes, in ditches along the side the road, ponds, and fish ponds all across the United States. You can recognize them because of their long slender leaves and the cattail at the top of the stalk. The cattail is a brown velvet color and bears the seed. The leaves of the cattail can be used to weave in baskets or for chair seats. Harvest them in the latter part of summer before the first frost. You can use a good sharp pair of scissors or knife to cut the leaves at the base where they touch the water. Lay the leaves flat to take home. You can use the leaves right away to weave, but it is better to dry them completely first. The leaves shrink a great deal if they have not dried completely. As soon as you get them back to your home, separate the leaves from the bundle if you did not do it while harvesting. Lay them out to dry. When completely dry, bundle the leaves and store until ready to use.

I have learned a lot about natural materials by being a member of online groups. Some of the Yahoo® groups I belong to are the Naturals group, Pine Needles group, Basketweaving group, and the Gourdpatch. Kathy Hoetlz, from the Pine Needles group, gave the following information on cattails and also gave me permission to use it in this book. "July is the best time to start cutting them. At this time they've reached their ultimate height for the summer and will not have started to brown on the leafy

Cattail leaves growing in Nancy Basket's pond. *Photography by Kelly Hazel.*

ends. Cut the plants close to the waterline. Split the leafy stems from the blunt end and not the pointed end, and, of course, discard the ant-eaten or chewed leaves as you harvest them. With the cattails, you would be using just the leafy part, not using the brown cylindrical flower part. Those are part of the round flower stem. The leafy cattail leaves should be pretty stable once they're coiled and shouldn't be shredding. A way to protect the leaves as you are coiling and adding them is to slightly twist the coil as you're working. This controls the lengths and makes a smoother surface. Separate the leafy stems from the round core that will carry the flower end. The leaves will be slippery and juicy. Wipe them off with a damp towel. Lay the leafy stems out in single layers to dry—in the shade they will keep their green color. I've read that you can use the round stems flattened and split. The leafy stems can be split lengthwise using a sewing pin. They split nicely, and can be split into quite narrow lengths. The curved bases of the leaves are usually trimmed off and not used. After they're thoroughly dry, they have to be moistened to use. It doesn't take much to dampen them. Rolling them in a damp towel will sometimes be enough. Because the leaves can retain a lot of water you should flatten them by pulling them through your fingers or, if you have an old wringer from a washing machine, running them through that. The idea is to expel as much water and air as possible. Their great length makes them ideal for coiling. I've not tried dyeing them, but their beautiful color is plenty for me. My experience with cattails has been using them as you would pine needles, as the core over which you stitch, known as 'open coiling'. I've seen baskets with the cattails used as binder as you would sinew. Those are 'closed coil' where the binder (cattail) is wrapped around the coil and covers it completely. As you start a new piece of cattail binder, you overlap the end of the old binder with the beginning of the new and continue wrapping the coil. It's important to keep the cattails straight while you are drying them. A bend or break in the leafy stem will crack and break while you're using it. That isn't so much a problem with the open coil method—you just add the pieces to the coil as you would pine needles. With the closed coil method, the cattails will break off. Keeping the cattails moist, not wet, will prevent problems. Cattails are a wonderful addition to our always interesting and growing collection of coiling materials."

Nancy Basket uses cattails for weaving and grows them in her pond. This is what she said about cattails. "Gather when they are the longest in your area by simply cutting with a sharp knife. Dried out of the sun, they retain a light green color. Their long, slender leaves grow like a hand attached under the water. Cut so you get all the leaves together. When they are pulled apart you can eat the celery-like white ends. You need to gather bunches for the winter. They become brittle and break the longer they stand in the weather. Tie raffia or cord around the middle of the stook (stalk), not too tightly, and stand them up with the larger ends down so they can drain. If not, they mold! Spritz them a bit or roll them in a moist towel so they mellow before using. This material is very hardy when coiled. A large basket I made in the shape of an egg basket, in the late eighties, is still very functional. The handle was changed once and replaced with a braided kudzu rim. The basket carried heavy loads and wore the fibers out over time."

Cattail leaf basket made by Nancy Basket. Handle is braided kudzu and it is filled with indigo dyed kudzu. *Photography by Kelly Hazel.*

Rushes and Bulrush

There are different varieties of bulrushes. They are perennial plants that can grow ten feet tall in moist soils. They grow in dense clumps in marshes and wetlands, and the leaves are dark green. According to the Free Dictionary by Farlex, an online dictionary, the definition of bulrush is "tall marsh plant with cylindrical seed heads that explode when mature shedding large quantities of down; its long flat leaves are used for making mats and chair seats; of North America, Europe, Asia, and North Africa." Bulrush is best cut in the summer.

Nancy Basket has bulrush growing in her pond. She gave me some information about using bulrush in weaving. "This plant needs to be dried first before using it or it shrinks and the coils are loose. They are a round plant and have a seed head on them that can be incorporated into the coils for texture. Cut close to the bottoms of individual strands with sharp scissors and dry as you would cattails. There are at least a thousand varieties of bulrush. Bulrushes grow in salt marshes, fresh water, and wet ditches. Some are tall and hard with more core than others. There are miniature versions growing close to the ground, as well. Bulrush was the original plant material used for wicker work until the invention of twisted paper. Reconstitute a few strands of bulrush and twist them together at different places, but not all at once in the same place. They can then be coiled on to gourds or used in baskets."

Natural rush is made from cattails or bulrushes. The rushes are harvested in early fall and dried. When they are ready for weaving, the rush must be soaked for a short time in hot water and then wrapped in damp towels to mellow. You must get the water out of the rush by wringing them out. You can also scrape the leaves with a sharp knife. The leaves can then be twisted in ropes and can be used to weave chair seats or weaving.

From top:
Bulrush growing in Nancy Basket's pond.
Photography by Kelly Hazel.

Mini bulrush growing in Nancy Basket's pond.
Photography by Kelly Hazel.

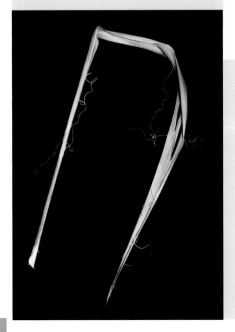

Yucca growing in Nancy Basket's yard. *Photography by Kelly Hazel.*

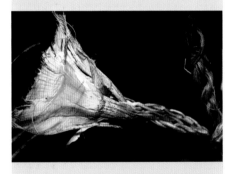

Cordage from yucca, daylily, papyrus. Bright yellow is the base of the yucca. *Courtesy of Nancy Gildersleeve. Photography by Kelly Hazel.*

Yucca

There are about forty species of yucca. It is a relative of the agave, a succulent used in many home gardens. Spanish Dagger Yucca grows in arid regions of the southwest. It is an evergreen plant with spine-tipped leaves that grow in a rosette around a thickened, central stem. The tough leaves are slit into fibers and used for weaving. There are some frost resistant species that can grow even in the northern parts of the United States. All the species like full sun and good drainage. Nancy Gildersleeve reports there are varieties growing in the wild in Florida. This plant, also called Adam's needle, is native to southeastern North America from North Carolina to Florida and west to Tennessee and Mississippi. It grows in dry, sandy areas and is used in many home landscapes.

In California, the Yucca whipplei fibers are used for coiling. When in bloom, the plant has a large cluster of white flowers. The plant blooms once and then dies. It could be considered a perennial because the seeds are dispersed and also produces offshoots around the old roots. It is the only yucca in the agave family that grows in California. The Native Americans in the western part of the United States in primitive times used the fibers from yucca and agave plants to make sandals to use when walking on the rocky terrain. They would beat the leaves on flat rocks to extract the tough fibers. The fibers were also made into cordage. Today some weavers in California use the stalk, when it falls over, as a base for coiling.

Pamela Zimmerman, who lives in North Carolina, uses processed yucca fibers for some of her creations. Here is how she processes the yucca. "Collect green yucca leaves from the bottom of the plant. Any yucca will do, but use caution with Spanish Dagger varieties. The best is the Yucca filamentosa, which is softer and has little white fibers escaping from the edges. Hackle leaves by drawing them through an old fashioned floral pin frog. Wear heavy gloves and push the leaf down into the tines while drawing the leaf towards you. It is possible to hackle (shred) through the fluted heads of the leaves, or stop at the head and leave it intact for a different look. Bundle in small bundles and hang to dry. It can be bleached, dyed, or used as-is. May be used dry, or dunked in water, as it moistens up very quickly. Do not soak. The fiber can also be retted. Most people coil with this fiber. Used in my pieces "Uprooted," (twined) and "Incubation" (coiled).

Bear grass or Yucca filamentosa. Notice the curly hairs on edges. *Courtesy of Nancy Gildersleeve. Photography by Kelly Hazel.*

Yucca pods. *Courtesy of Sandy Phillips, Heart Song Gourd Art.*

Unicorn Plant

The unicorn plant is also known as devil's claw. It grows no taller than three feet tall and loves rich woods, slopes, and moist meadows. Gloria Small gave me the following information: "I grow devil's claw, also known as the unicorn plant. They are annual plants that come back each year from seed. They grow a seed pod that splits in half when mature and drying—this is the devils claw and rightfully named as the tip is sharp and fetching, will grab you if you brush past it and sticks like the devil. I always grow the claws and keep them on hand to craft and sell. This is a fun plant to grow!"

Terri Schmit, from Wisconsin, uses devil's claw. "These are usually found in the southwest, but several years ago I planted some of these seeds in Wisconsin and they grew. Devil's claw produces a spectacular plant. The claw itself, when grown in this climate, is huge, some are up to 18 inches long. Devil's claw dries naturally but needs to be 'peeled' before they can be used. The peel comes off quite easily. I like to sand my claws smooth and sometimes paint them as they accept spray paint very well. Most of the time when I use them, I cut the seed pod off and use just the claw; however, the pod itself is quite an amazing natural embellishment. I usually coil them onto a gourd by simply trying different combinations of claws until I find something that works with the shape of my gourd. However, it's very easy to manipulate the shape of the claw by simply soaking it first, then you can bend it just about any way you want."

Karen Hafer, from Maryland, uses devil's claw on her gourd art and shared the following information. "The devil's claw got its name because its fruit will readily cling to animals' hooves or your shoes if you should step on them. The plant is also called the 'unicorn plant', since the pod is hornlike before it splits open. Many Native American tribes of the southwest still use the green or dried pods today for food and in basketry." A tutorial using devil's claw on gourds is included in Section 2.7.

Co-Motion by Terri Schmit was woven with devil's claw. *Courtesy of Terri Schmit.*

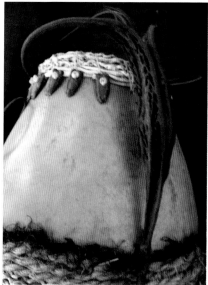

Close up of Karen Hafer's gourd using devil's claw on the rim. *Courtesy of Karen Hafer.*

Incubation by Pamela Zimmerman; dyed yucca fiber, hibiscus fiber, polymer clay, paint, gourd pieces, modeling compound, resins, waxed linen, and freshwater pearls. The yucca in this is coiled. *Photography by Ronald L. Sowers Photography.*

Uprooted by Pamela Zimmerman is woven with dandelion stems, processed yucca fiber, hardwood tree roots with dirt, palm inflorescence, waxed linen, round reed, and copper. The yucca in this is twined. *Photography by Ronald L. Sowers Photography.*

Canes and Bamboo

River Cane

River cane grows like other bamboo. New cane sprouts up from underground runners. River cane and switch cane, a smaller cane, are the only bamboos native to the United States. They both grow in bottomlands near rivers and streams. At one time, river cane grew in the South so thick you could hardly get between the plants. At one time river cane was an essential resource for the Cherokee and other southeastern tribes. The Cherokee made strong baskets by splitting the canes and dyeing them. Today the river cane has dwindled. Now cane only exists in the fringes of fields and sparsely scattered along creeks and rivers. The Cherokee, today, have a difficult time finding cane for their baskets due to increased population, pollution, and other factors that have taken natural cane-friendly lands. The Land Trust for the Little Tennessee (LTLT) is successfully managing a river cane restoration project along the Little Tennessee River near Franklin, North Carolina. They are experimenting with different plants and techniques for growing the river cane.

Making cane baskets are very time consuming. First, you harvest the cane. It is ready for harvest when it reaches about eight feet tall and is about as thick as your thumb. The Cherokee harvest process involves the following steps: cutting, splitting, peeling, trimming, and dyeing. After the cane is harvested it is split lengthwise into four pieces and then scraped to leave the shiny outer surface. The cane is dyed using natural dyes. From Weaving Wildly: Mats and Baskets the Choctaw Way by Mary Lou Stahl, the process of peeling is described: "With the help of a very big sharp knife, the outer layer is peeled off these quarter lengths of cane by inserting the knife blade and drawing it steadily down the cane toward the person. This takes skill and strength. The object is to obtain a strong, flexible strip of even thickness. The sides are trimmed for a uniform width and the strips are scraped on the inner surface to reduce thickness making them more flexible." There is also a good explanation of how to process cane in Cherokee Basketry, by M. Anna Farielloo. Nancy Basket gave me several pieces of river cane. I tried to split it into pieces thin enough to weave with. It was very difficult to do. My splints are still too thick and crude, nothing like the splints the Cherokee use to make their baskets. This gave me a greater appreciation of the native cane baskets.

Nancy Basket gave me some river cane and I took it home to try and split. It is not an easy job. *Photography by Kelly Hazel.*

Small Cherokee river cane basket in author's collection. Artist unknown. *Photography by Kelly Hazel.*

Bamboo

Bamboo is much larger than the river cane. It is a tough material. The Chinese and Indonesian culture have made bamboo baskets throughout history. Bamboo grows in just about every country in the world. To use bamboo as a weaving material, the stalk must be cut in sections and split several times. The pieces are then separated into smaller splits and cut to appropriate lengths. A large sharp knife or machete is needed to split the tough bamboo pieces lengthwise. Polly Jacobs Giacchina, from southern California, uses bamboo and date palm in her sculptural forms. Polly describes how she collects and prepares the bamboo. "Bamboo is collected either from the smaller plants I have on my property or collected from other gardens. It can also be bought from suppliers, depending on the size and type needed for the project. Bamboo is a very strong, rigid material. The individual poles can be divided and trimmed down into strips or used whole. Bamboo can only be bent by using a heating method. I use a heat gun to gently coax the bamboo into a desired bent position. Each piece of bamboo must be bent individually."

I have a basket in my collection from Chiang Mai, the largest and most culturally significant city in northern Thailand. It is woven with bamboo and has a dark lacquer applied to the outside of the basket. Weaving in Thailand has been practiced for hundreds of years and has been passed on from one generation to another. Bamboo is the main material used for weaving.

Meditative Path (detail) by Polly Jacobs Giacchina: Date palm and washi paper on timber bamboo, 41" x 4 1/2" x 4". *Photography by Rodney Nakamoto.*

Close up of weaving in bamboo basket. Unknown artist. *Photography by Kelly Hazel.*

Basket made of bamboo in author's collection. It came from Chiang Mai, Thailand. Unknown artist. *Photography by Kelly Hazel.*

Bamboo basket from author's collection. *Photography by Kelly Hazel.*

Shoreline (detail) by Polly Jacobs Giacchina: Date palm, bamboo, and random weave caning 18" x 12" x 10". *Photography by Rodney Nakamoto.*

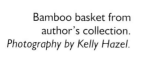

Karen Hafer's *Devil's Claw Gourd* is also woven in the center with date palm fruit stalks, yarn, jute, unraveled seagrass, and split palm leaves (dried). *Courtesy of Karen Hafer.*

An antler basket made by Angie Craft. It uses corn husks for the rim. *Photography by Kelly Hazel.*

Umbrella plant or umbrella papyrus that I saw in Charlotte Durrence's back yard. *Photography by Derral Durrence.*

Other Plants

There are many other plants that can be used for weaving and coiling. Natural fibers that come from different plants are desirable for use in weaving. The umbrella plant or umbrella papyrus can be grown in water gardens in warmer climates as found in Florida. I saw an umbrella plant growing in Charlotte Durrence's back yard. Floridian Nancy Gildersleeve uses this plant to coil baskets. Hemp is a fiber that comes from the Cannabis plant. Hemp fiber is a long, strong, and absorbent material that is ideal for twining. This twining fiber is obtained when the plant begins to flower. Rope is also made from hemp. Jute comes from a plant. In Bengal and in the entire southwest of Bangladesh, the white jute plant is used to make rope.

Roots of plants are used for weaving and making cordage. The roots of the horsetail are very black. In fact, it is one of nature's few natural black fibers. They grow very deep in the soil and it takes a lot of work to harvest them. It is the root cover that is used for weaving. Since it is segmented, it is difficult to get enough fiber to be useful. The segments are short and the covering has to be pulled or scraped from the root. Maidenhair fern can also be used for weaving. The fern stems are black and shiny.

Cornhusk is another suitable material used for weaving. When harvesting corn, the husks can be harvested and saved for weaving. Separate the husks from the corn and allow to dry. If dried in the shade, they will retain some of the green color. If dried in sun, it will be an off-white. The husks sold in grocery stores have been bleached white. Dip husks in water for about five minutes and wrap in a towel to mellow. They are tough and can be shredded, curled, twisted, stitched, and flattened. For many years, the settlers in the Appalachian mountain areas have made corn husk dolls. Nancy Basket shared the following information. "Take corn husks from around the cob and let dry inside for a few days. They can be bundled up and stored for later. They are easily split and can be braided into long lengths, then sewn on gourds or made into baskets. Barely moisten the husks before using them. They can be twisted into coils and take dyes well. Native people from the northeast used braided lengths for cornhusk masks in some of their ceremonies. Salt baskets were woven from this material, also a type of moccasin."

Another plant I use for decoration, but have also woven in my gourd baskets is philodendron. It is the large variety that grows in Florida and other tropical regions called split leaf philodendron. It is the sheath that falls off the new leaf shoot. It has tough fibers and can be used in weaving and coiling. The sheaths range in size from six inches to twenty inches. The colors will vary from brown to a rust color. I store mine in paper bags until I am ready to use them. When ready to use the sheath, I place it in warm water for about thirty minutes. If the sheath is very large, it may take longer. You can also soak for five minutes and then put in a towel to mellow. I have many friends in Florida who bring sheaths to me. In fact, in Florida, it is considered yard waste. Last, I will mention lavender. Lavender is so calming and smells wonderful. Weave it in your baskets as accent. I have a lavender wand that a friend made for me and I lay it on my pillow at night. So, you can see there are weaving and coiling plants in just about every section of the United States. Go out in nature and look around for plants that can be used and experiment.

Corn husks can be used for weaving. *Photography by Kelly Hazel.*

Papyrus stem cordage stitched with artificial sinew; coaster about two inches and made by Nancy Gildersleeve. *Photography by Kelly Hazel.*

Nancy Gildersleeve made this rim of corn, palm, yucca, cornhusk, and daylily cordage, catalpa pod, philodendron, and a palm leaf boondoggle (square braid) and rose. *Photography by Kelly Hazel.*

Horsetail equisetum grows in Nancy Basket's pond. The roots of the horsetail are very black. In fact it is one of nature's few natural black fibers and can be woven into baskets. *Courtesy of Nancy Basket. Photography by Kelly Hazel.*

Philodendron sheath can be woven in baskets or used as a rim for a gourd. *Photography by Kelly Hazel.*

Lavender gives a nice smell when woven in a basket. This lavender plant grows in the author's front yard. *Photography by Kelly Hazel.*

1.6: Grasses

There are so many grasses that are used to weave baskets. People all over the world use readily available materials. In Ghana, elephant grass and savannah grass is used for making baskets. Aboriginal weaving grass, *Myoporum parvifolium*, is used by Australian Aborigines for weaving. In India, sikki grass grows in wet, marshy areas around the rivers. It is a golden grass that is collected during the rainy season and used for making baskets. In Bangladesh, natural woven baskets are made from sturdy kaisa grass. Kaisa grass dries from its natural light green to a very pale, almost tan. Native Americans in Oregon, Washington state, and British Columbia have traditionally made beautiful baskets with bear grass. Northwest coast Indians used swamp grass to create their baskets. Some varieties in use over the years and still today are switchgrass, feather grass, and broom corn millet. These grasses are used as core for coiling and stitching and weft in twining. As with many other natural materials, you need to experiment. Most grasses are cut and put in the sun to dry. Some grasses can be dyed to add color to your baskets. Below are some common grasses used for weaving and coiling.

This tiny lidded basket, Mayan from Belize, is made of a local grass. Unknown artist. *Courtesy of Nancy Gildersleeve. Photography by Kelly Hazel.*

Grass basket made in Bangladesh and in the author's collection. Unknown artist. *Photography by Kelly Hazel.*

Basket made in Charleston in the style of the bulrush African baskets. Unknown artist. *Photography by Kelly Hazel.*

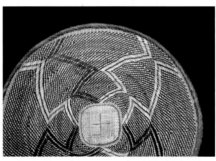

African basket made on a coffee plantation. Grasses and bulrush was used to make the basket. Unknown artist. *Photography by Kelly Hazel.*

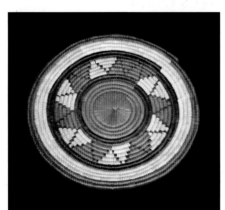

Native American coiled basket made with grasses in author's collection. *Photography by Kelly Hazel.*

Sweetgrass

Sweetgrass is a winter-hardy perennial grass, normally found growing in rich, moist soils. In my research I found two different kinds of sweetgrass. One is *Hierochloe odorata* and has a sweet, long-lasting aroma that reminds you of the smell of vanilla. It is found in the northern parts of the United States around the Great Lakes and also in Canada. Other names for the sweetgrass are holy grass, vanilla grass, bluejoint, buffalo grass, and zebrovka. Sweetgrass is traditionally harvested in late June or early July, although it can be harvested any time during the growing season. If you harvest it after the first frost, it has little scent. In the wild, it grows among other grasses instead of pure stands of sweetgrass. Make sure you cut it about an inch above the ground level. If it is pulled out by the root, the sweetgrass can be severely damaged and takes much longer to recover. Many Native American tribes in North America use sweetgrass as part of their prayers. It has also been used for medicine. The Native Americans weave sweetgrass in their baskets. The Ojibwa make boxes from white birch bark, bind the edges with sweetgrass, and decorate with quills. After cutting the grass, place it in the sun to dry, turning the leaves often. When the leaf tips start to curl (about 30 to 45 minutes) place the grass in the shade until it is completely dry. If it dries completely in the sun, you will lose some of the aroma. You can store the grasses by bundling them and hanging in a dry place. If you want to keep the scent longer, layer completely dry grass between newspaper and put them a strong plastic bag. You can put the bags in the freezer to keep the scent even longer.

I am more familiar with the southern sweetgrass since I live in South Carolina. This sweetgrass does not have a vanilla odor, but smells like fresh hay. Sweetgrass grows in the southern part of the United States, extending from North Carolina to Texas. It is a native, perennial warm season grass that is found in coastal dunes. The grass is harvested in spring and summer by "pullers," who slip the grass out of its roots. The fresh grass is put in the sun to dry for several days to several weeks. It is then bundled and placed in a dry place to store. You can grow your own sweetgrass. There are many suppliers who sell the seed or a plug for planting.

Angie Wagner, from Kempton, Pennsylvania, grows sweetgrass (*Hierochloe odorata*) at her farm and sent pictures of it growing. *Courtesy of Angie Wagner.*

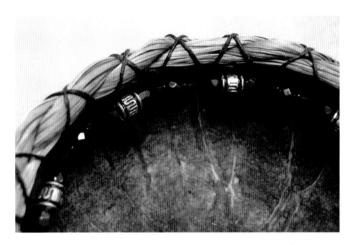

Angie Wagner uses sweetgrass for coiling on a gourd and also as a filler in basket rims. *Courtesy of Angie Wagner.*

Sweetgrass baskets in author's collection were made in Charleston, South Carolina. Artists unknown. *Photography by Kelly Hazel.*

I have many sweetgrass baskets in my personal collection. I have also taken a sweetgrass basket making class with a wonderful weaver from the lower part of the state. She looked at some of my baskets and told me that some of them have museum quality patina. Some of these baskets were purchased many years ago by my husband's parents when they took a trip to Charleston, South Carolina. I have them displayed in a prominent place in my home. Sweetgrass basket making is a traditional art form brought to America by slaves who came from Africa, and this art form has been passed down from generation to generation. For more than 300 years, sweetgrass baskets have been made in Charleston and Mt. Pleasant, South Carolina. During the days of slavery these baskets were used for agricultural purposes. The plantation owners would sell the baskets to other plantation owners to use for collecting vegetables and even cotton from the fields. The sweetgrass baskets made by the Gullah people are coil-sewn instead of twined or plaited. The common material for the coil in earlier times was bulrush. The coils were stitched together with white oak strips or strips from the saw palmetto tree. Today, they use sweetgrass and long leaf pine needle coils and stitch them together with sable palmetto palm leaves.

Many years ago I talked to one of the ladies along Route 17 coming from Mount Pleasant and she told me her "tool" for opening up the rows of coiling was a silver teaspoon passed down from generation to generation. She said the spoon (called "nailbone") has the handle cut off, and the end is sanded and sharpened. So the tool is actually an antique article, but such tools are highly prized by their owners. She also told me that the art form is dying out because the young people do not want to do the baskets any more. It is also hard to find the sweetgrass because of so much residential development being done along coastal islands and marshlands. The area where sweetgrass grows and could be harvested is disappearing, because of the private property restrictions. They have to go as far as Florida to collect the sweetgrass. Many of them pay collectors to get the grass for them. The USDA Forest Service, the College of Charleston, the South Carolina Sea Grant Consortium, and several community groups have formed a partnership to restore habitats containing sweetgrass. South Carolina's Governor Mark Sanford, in 2010, designated sweetgrass baskets as the state's official Low Country handcraft. Communities have taken measures to preserve the art form and protect the sweetgrass harvests.

Loose sweetgrass and palmetto leaves used to make sweetgrass baskets. *Photography by Kelly Hazel.*

Seagrass

Seagrasses are the underwater flowering plants that live in protected bays, lagoons, and other shallow coastal waters. It is not seaweed. Seagrass needs sunlight in order to photosynthesize. It has roots, leaves, flowers, and seeds, just like land plants. There are fifty-two different species around the world. Florida has seven varieties in lagoons and bays throughout the state. You can cut the seagrass and dry it much like the sweetgrass. It can also be dyed with as little water as possible and concentrated dye. It will take a little longer for the dye to absorb than for other weaving materials. You can purchase seagrass in individual strands or woven into ropes of various sizes. Some of the seagrass ropes sold are actually made of land grown grasses. Some are actually sedges that grow in marshy areas. The grass is light green or tan in color. Much of the seagrass sold by suppliers come from Hong Kong where they commercially grow it in patties flooded with water. You can also buy dyed seagrass from some suppliers.

Angie Wagner of the Country Seat posted on the Pine Needles group her method for dying seagrass. "I used to measure it out into fifty foot bundles and dye the small amounts, but it kinked worse and I would have to recoil them after they dried. I started dyeing the full three pound coils of seagrass. I put several very long twist-ties around the coil, loosely, so the coil could expand in the dye bath and the strands could loosen and move around. Then I cut the ties that hold it tightly together. Seagrass takes a long time to dye so it often stays in the dye bath for 1-2 hours. I poke it with a stick occasionally and flip it over to make sure it is all dyeing evenly. It still kinks, but it seems to stay more contained this way. So far I've only had one coil (and I've dyed a lot) that didn't dye properly in the center. I think I had the twist-ties on too tightly. As it dries, I measure it out into the fifty foot bundles. It's easier to measure out the seagrass while it's damp since the dry ends cut into my hands, I've worn holes in gloves when measuring it out dry."

Seagrass rope coils purchased from a supplier. *Photography by Kelly Hazel.*

Loose seagrass. *Photography by Kelly Hazel.*

Maxine Riley made a basket using flat seagrass braid for the top part. *Photography by Kelly Hazel.*

Broomcorn and Broomsedge

Broomcorn, *Sorghum vulgare* var. *technicum*, originated in Africa. It was introduced by Benjamin Franklin in the United States in the early 1700s. According to the Departments of Agronomy, Soil Science, and Plant Pathology, College of Agricultural and Life Sciences and Cooperative Extension Service, University of Wisconsin-Madison," Initially, broomcorn was grown only as a garden crop for use in the home. By 1834 commercial broomcorn production had spread to several states in the Northeast and started moving west. Illinois was the leading producer of broomcorn in the 1860s, but production of the crop in that state virtually ceased in 1967. Some production has occurred in Wisconsin since 1948." It was used for making brooms because the fibers were straight and pliable. It can be grown in just about every state. It does best in warm, fertile soils. There are three varieties grown in the United States: standard, western dwarf, and whisk dwarf. When the entire brush is green from the tip down to the base, it is time to harvest. Lay it on slats in sheds for ten to twenty days to cure. I have a friend who grows broomcorn in Greenville, South Carolina. She works at the Roper Mountain Science Center and demonstrates broom making. I have received broomcorn from her and used it for weaving in my rib baskets.

Broomsedge, *Andropogon spp*, is also known as beard grass. The long brush-like grasses were used to make brooms. It is a perennial bunch grass that grows about three to four feet. It dies back in the fall and comes back out in the spring. It grows throughout much of the eastern United States, from as far north as Maine and south into Florida. It is a good material to weave into your baskets or weave on a gourd. Cut it close to the ground after the seeds fall off. This happens in late fall. Bundle it and store in a dry place.

Turkey broom made by the author. It was made with broom corn. *Photography by Kelly Hazel.*

Gourd, blue inside is leather dye. Top trimmed with broom corn, palm, yucca, cornhusk, and daylily cordage, catalpa pod, philodendron. *Courtesy of Nancy Gildersleeve. Photograph by Kelly Hazel.*

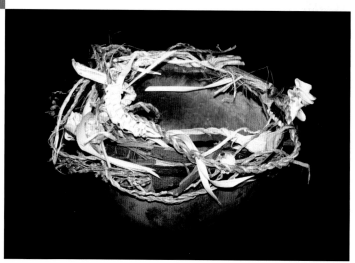

1.7: Barks

Polly Adams Sutton uses cedar bark for her baskets. She shared, "I gather my own cedar bark from logging areas and prep it myself. I split the outer bark off in the forest and bring home the inner bark to dry out. I resoak it, cut, and split it for weaving. I use wire to twine with, the spokes are cedar and the weavers are usually ash or cane." After taking a basket class from Cass Schorsch at a convention, I decided to start using barks in my gourd weavings. Barks add a new dimension and texture to baskets and on gourds. Cass Schorsch knows more about barks than any weaver I know. She allowed me to use her detailed information about harvesting tree barks for basketry.

Cass told me how she harvests cedar bark. "Every Spring, for the last twenty-five years, you could always find me in the woods harvesting different tree barks for the following year's teaching assignments. Starting the first of May, I would travel to the Upper Peninsula to harvest cedar bark. This is done by finding a nice straight tree with no branches for at least eight feet. The diameter of these trees is usually 12" to 15". After cutting the tree down, I would then make two slits about 4" apart with my knife. I use what is called a 'sheepsfoot bladed knife'. You could also use a tile knife. After cutting the two slits, you want to get under the bark to loosen it, then grab that piece and pull. The first three to four pulls will 'V' off the log. The bark is

Cambium by Polly Adams Sutton, 14" x 10" x 7 1/2". The basket was made with cedar bark, cane, and wire. *Courtesy of Polly Adams Sutton.*

In the spring, when the sap is up in the trees, Cass Schorsch and her partner Jack go to the upper peninsula to harvest cedar bark. *Courtesy of Cass Schorsch.*

Jack strips the bark from the log. *Courtesy of Cass Schorsch.*

Cass is separating the outer bark from the inner bark. *Photography by Jack Mickevich.*

Cass splitting the cedar to make thinner splits. *Courtesy of Cass Schorsch. Photography by Jack Mickevich.*

Using branches from the trees that have been cut, Cass and Jack haul the strips of bark out of the woods. *Courtesy of Cass Schorsch. Photography by Jack Mickevich.*

One year's harvest will take two to three weeks to dry. Then it is stored for a year before it is used. That allows any sap that might be in the bark to come to the surface making it easier to rub off. All the coils will be split one more time, allowing both sides to be used. *Courtesy of Cass Schorsch.*

actually trying to find the grain. Usually the fourth to fifth pull, the width of the strip will be the same at the top as the slit you made at the bottom. As cedar likes to twist as it grows, you will find this true when pulling the bark. Next you want to split the outer bark from the inner bark. No sense in carrying out of the woods what you aren't going to use. Taking each strip, you will make a sharp bend about 6" from the end of the strip. Holding each side of the split, you will start separating the outer from the inner bark. The most important thing to remember when doing this is 'pull to the thicker side of the split'. It also helps to hold the strip between your legs when splitting, which gives you more leverage. When finished, coil your strips and tie with some scrap cedar. This allows them to dry in this shape, thereby making it easy to put them in a bucket to soak when you get ready to use them. (The trees are propped up off the ground and left in the woods to dry somewhat. In August, the owner of the land will haul the logs out to be milled for lumber. Sometimes the logs have been used to make cedar furniture.) The most important thing is to get your cedar dry. I do this by putting all the coils on a tarp, which allows me to pull it out in the sunshine during the day, then pull it back in the garage for the night, thus eliminating dew from forming and getting the bark wet again. There is nothing worse than mold on your bark when it is black. It cannot be removed. When you are ready to weave with your cedar, you will have to soak it in warm water for thirty minutes, then wrap in a wet towel for five to six hours, allowing it to mellow. Using your knife, make a slit at one end. Bend the bark in half, which will help the layers separate. Now take the two sides in each hand and again 'pull to the thicker side' and split the strip in half. Now you are ready to cut your strips into widths you want for weaving."

Cass also gave me information on harvesting and preparing birch bark. "Harvesting birch bark should be done in the middle of summer. You do not have to cut the tree down to get a couple of sheets of bark from the tree. When looking for a tree, you always want to walk around the entire tree before making your first cut. The weather prevailing side of the tree might be very crusty. If the rest of the tree is beautiful, then you should make your vertical cut through the weather prevailing side. This side of the tree has thinner bark, which you would not want in the middle of your weaving strips. Do not girdle the tree. There is no reason to make any cuts but the one vertical cut the length of the piece you want. At this time of the year, when you make your cut, the bark will almost pop off the tree. Get underneath the bark and walk around the tree while pulling off the bark. Now here is the most important part of this whole process. Get the sheet you just pulled off and lay it flat on the ground. Use logs or whatever you might have brought along as a weight. I always took about four bricks with me to the harvesting site. Birch bark wants to curl in the opposite direction it was on the tree. You will never get this curl out. Birch bark has memory. I store all my birch bark in presses, similar to flower presses, only much larger. When it is time to split the bark, I take the end of the sheet and roll it over my finger. Mother Nature will usually give you a split. Go with it. Again remember to always pull to the thicker side. Some pieces you can split three to four times. Just don't get it so thin it becomes unusable. Always cut your strips parallel to the lenticels (lines) in the bark."

Cass also wrote about harvesting other barks. "Some of the barks I harvest every year are white pine and red pine. These trees I have came from tree farmers. After so many years, the farmers will go through and cut every other row of trees down. Those are the trees I get. With the white pine, you want to cut the whorls of branches off, leaving you with a nice log. Depending on the weather in previous years, some of the logs will be long and some short. First thing you want to do is scrub your logs in order to get the environmental dirt off. Now take your knife down the length of the log and simply roll the log off the bark. I have used white pine for folded bowls and have cut it in strips to use for weaving. I usually weave over something as the bark is fragile when cut in narrow strips. This could be a glass vase or another basket. Red pine is the same as white. Again you want to cut the whorls of branches off your logs. You will have to take some of the outer bark off with a draw knife. Then cut strips from one end of the log to the other and pull them off. Next is 'pop and peel'. This is done by rolling the bark over your finger, which makes it pop, then you can peel that piece off. It is somewhat time consuming but worth the effort."

The plaited baskets in this picture are birch bark baskets woven by Angie Wagner. She uses a combination of Russian birch bark from Vladimir Yarish and bark that she harvested locally in Kempton, Pennsylvania. *Courtesy of Angie Wagner.*

Close up of a birch bark basket made by the author. *Photograph by Kelly Hazel.*

Close up of an Alaskan birch bark basket in the author's collection. Artist unknown. *Photograph by Kelly Hazel.*

Undercurrents. Woven with reed and barks in undulating rows. *Courtesy of Cass Schorsch. Scanned by Kelly Hazel.*

Slant Bark by Don Weeke, 23" x 14.5" x 15", 2009. Oak branch, eucalyptus bark, reed, king palm seed frond; techniques: Weaving, joinery. *Courtesy of Don Weeke. Photography by Tom Henderson.*

Spruce bark is one of Cass' favorite barks. She said, "Spruce bark has so much character, which makes for wonderful focal points in your weaving. I usually harvest branches as it is easier to work with and not so thick. After cutting the branch off the tree, you want to cut all the little branches off the limb. Next, make a cut along one side of the branch, then another cut on the other side of the branch. Get underneath the bark at the end with your knife, then start pulling. Always pull in the direction the little branches were growing off the limb. Then you will end up with all these beautiful little knot holes. If you pull in the wrong direction, you will tear the bark where the little branches were. I live in an area where Christmas trees are a crop. If you develop a friendship with the farmer, it is always fun to go pulling 'roots'. By going to a Christmas tree farm, you can go between the rows to pull. This will not hurt the trees. The roots can be split and by going in the spring, you can pull the bark off with your gloves. There are so many trees out there that have usable bark: hickory, mulberry, poplar, tulip poplar. The list is endless. If you want to know if you can use a tree bark and not have to cut the tree down to find out, do the following: go up to a tree in the spring and make a cut with your knife about 6 inches long and 1/2 inch wide. Pull the bark off. Now roll it around your finger. If the bark does not crack and break, you can use it. If the outer bark cracks, but not the inner, then you know you will have to take the outer bark off and just use the inner bark. If they both crack and break, then you know it is not usable and you saved a tree from being cut down."

The other tree Cass enjoys harvesting is basswood. "I usually stick to small trees, no bigger than 12 inches in diameter. Cut the tree down and take the outer bark off with a drawknife. It is almost like peeling a cucumber. Now cut strips about four inches wide and pull the bark off. You will notice that it is much thicker than you anticipated. Take all these strips and soak them in a pond or water trough for four to six weeks. After this amount of time, you will notice the layers coming apart. Remove the log from the pond and immediately put it in a bleach bath overnight. This will stop the bacterial action and help eliminate the rotting odor. I take all the strips and hang them over the clothesline. Then the magical part: separating all the layers, of which there will be many. Basswood makes some of the most beautiful cordage, and one tree will be enough to last you a lifetime. The touch, the smell, and the sound of the layers blowing in the breeze as you separate them are a wonderful experience. Always get permission wherever you go to harvest. You would be surprised how cooperative the Department of Natural Resources can be when they find out what you want to do. Most of my harvesting over the years has been from private land. Talk to people or run ads in the local newspaper. You will be surprised how cooperative people will be in trade for a basket. This basket came from MY tree. Have fun, dress properly, and above all, remember you are dealing with dangerous tools, from the chain saw on down to the pocket knife."

Don Weeke uses eucalyptus bark and oak branches that he gathers himself in his baskets and gourd art. "I clean off the outer bark, sand them down, and then treat them with lemon oil."

Nancy Gildersleeve uses hemlock bark and hickory bark in weaving baskets. The bark splints make a rustic, durable, and beautiful chair seat. Hickory is a traditional material used for weaving chair seats. You can buy many barks through suppliers if they are not located where you live.

While at the Florida retreat, Nancy Gildersleeve shared with me how to split cedar bark to make a thinner splint. She took a knife and inserted it at the end of the strip. Then she used her hands to hold the divided splints and pull them apart. If it gets thinner on one side, pull more on the other side. This will keep the pieces the same width.

Spruce bark basket made by Cass Schorsch. *Courtesy of Cass Schorsch. Scanned by Kelly Hazel.*

Small hemlock bark and yucca cordage basket made by Nancy Gildersleeve. Bark strips are about 3/8" wide. *Photograph by Kelly Hazel.*

Close up of a basket using hickory bark and seagrass rope. *Photograph by Kelly Hazel.*

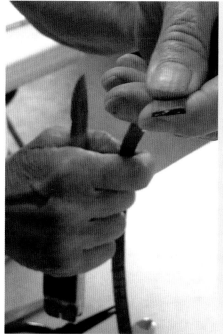

Nancy Gildersleeve starts splitting cedar bark by inserting a knife in the end to divide the bark. *Photography by Marianne Barnes.*

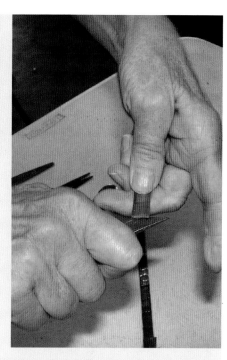

In splitting cedar bark, pull the bark apart evenly. *Photography by Marianne Barnes.*

In splitting cedar bark, keep your fingers close to the part that is being split. If the bark becomes too thin on one side, pull a little harder on the other side. *Photography by Marianne Barnes.*

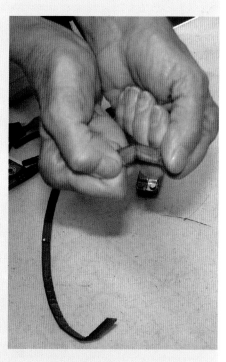

When the bark comes apart evenly, you have two nice pieces for weaving. *Photography by Marianne Barnes.*

Pieced Reflections (detail) by Polly Jacobs Giacchina is made of date palm, bamboo, and mosaic glass 17" x 12" x 8". *Photography by Rodney Nakamoto.*

1.8: Palms

Polly Jacobs Giacchina is an artist who uses date palm stems and bamboo. Here is what she had to say, "Sculptural forms and structures express my view of art. Weaving with natural materials allows me to respond to my surroundings and develop design ideas. Through this connection I emphasize works that are inspired by the textures, colors, and unique components of nature. I sculpt using the weaving technique, twining. Pliable natural and industrial materials are used to explore each project. Even the collecting of materials, mainly date palm, is part of the creative process. At times, multiple units are produced and then put together to form relationships. Stronger rigid materials are bent and reformed to seek new possibilities. Reinterpreting and transforming materials creates a more meaningful complex form, to transcend and connect to nature. My natural materials are growing in Southern California. I collect date palm by either pole trimming it from the tree or getting assistance from professional tree trimmers. The date palm tree that I prefer can be over fifty feet high. The weaving material is actually the flowering part of the tree, where the dates grow. The stalks are dried, trimmed from the main branch, soaked in water, and then used to weave. The date palm is a great weaving material that allows me the freedom to shape and obtain the sculptural forms I desire."

Don Weeke uses natural material with gourds to create his baskets and gourd art. The following is how he harvests his materials. "I collect and use the seed fronds of the date palm and king palm. After the fronds are thoroughly dried, I cut the palm sticks from the central stalk or frond. For weaving, I soak them in water until they become pliable enough to make the curve I need."

The seed fronds, also called palm inflorescence, come from a spathe (a modified leaf that forms a sheathe to enclose the flower cluster). The royal, queen, and coconut palms are known for their large spathe. Some palms do not have a spathe. In a coconut palm tree, the inflorescence emerges from the crown being surrounded and protected by a long, brownish, and semi-woody spathe, shaped like a long scoop. This spathe protects the flowers as they grow and stay on the tree even after the formation of mature coconuts. The spathe may be several feet long and quite woody. In fact, the fallen spathes of coconut palms, *Cocos nucifera*, can be boiled, dried, and waxed to produce a beautiful boat-shaped bowl. Coconut leaves from the coco palm tree are a flexible material used in forming baskets. The leaves are used whole for roofs and fences in the tropics. Bound together, the leaves can be fashioned into brooms and brushes. The leaves can be cut into strips and used to weave baskets. The sweetgrass baskets of

The rim of this gourd, made by Gail Bishop, was stitched with raffia. *Courtesy of Gail Bishop.*

Charleston are stitched with palm leaf, Sabal palmetto. The leaves are stripped into narrow lengths and used to attach the coils together. One of my online friends, Eve Elliott, who owns Botanical Booty, loves natural materials. "I am a yard waste queen. I am finding many ways to work with all parts of palm fronds. I also use the sticks that come from the fruiting inflorescence (the ugly branch that has all of the pollen flowers or the mini coconut-like seeds). The sticks have a lot of character. I weave with them to make a very primitive looking basket. I embellish them with leaf sheaths from the tree philodendrons."

The raffia palms are a group of twenty species of palms native to tropical regions of Africa, especially Madagascar. The membrane on the underside of each individual frond leaf is taken off to create a long, thin fiber, which can be dyed and woven as a textile into products ranging from hats to shoes to baskets. Raffia is also used to stitch coils together to make coiled baskets. Wraphia ribbon is made from raffia. In the project section there is a pattern for a Cherokee basket by Shirley Thomason. Shirley uses wraphia ribbon to secure her coils.

Palm seed fronds, also called palm inflorescence. *Photograph by Kelly Hazel.*

Diamond Linear by Don Weeke, 21 1/2" x 10" x 10", 2009. Reed, paint, king palm seed frond. Techniques are weaving, couching, and pyrography. *Courtesy of Don Weeke. Photography by Rodney Nakamoto.*

This is part of the sheathing bracts called spathes that covers the palm inflorescence. *Photograph by Kelly Hazel.*

Strips of palmetto leaves (*Sabal palmetto*) are used to stitch the coils of a sweetgrass basket. *Photograph by Kelly Hazel.*

1.9: Pine Needles

Brown and green long leaf pine needles from the south and the short one is ponderosa pine from California. *Photograph by Kelly Hazel.*

Unfinished pine needle basket with a clay base, made by Nancy Basket. *Photograph by Kelly Hazel.*

There are many varieties of pine needles. In the South we have the long leaf pine, Pinus palustris, and in the western part of the country you will find the Torrey pine, Pinus torreyana, that grows in southern California; canary pine, a landscaping pine that cannot tolerate cold temperatures; and ponderosa pine, a pine from Mexico that also grows in California and tolerates very high heat. In the following, some of my basket and gourd friends will tell you a little about the pine needles they use.

Long Leaf Pine

Long leaf pine has been around for a long time. It is a tall, stately pine that once covered millions of acres in the southeastern part of the United States coastal plain. It takes this pine 150 years to become full sized and they can live for 300 years. It is common to find them in flatwoods, sandhills, and upland hardwood areas. It can reach a height of 80 to 100 feet tall.

Nancy Basket has a history of making Cherokee pine needle baskets. Here is what she says about the long leaf pine. "Long leaf pines have needles that can grow to 24 inches long! That would be considered green gold as most basketry companies sell long leaf needles 12 to 18 inches long for about $25 a pound. This tree grows about 150 miles inland from the coasts of Virginia down to Louisiana. It is used for a southern ground cover, but don't think you can use the needles from a bale sold down here for about six dollars as they are all bent and broken. Sorting those needles would surely drive you to the institution from where it is said basketry is taught. For an interesting video go to *www.knowitall. org/naturalstate/html/acc-fa/N-Basket/Interview-n.cfm.* Forest Murphy, at the end of the video, shows me where to gather pine needles from the back of small trees in the sandhills' forest he helps manage. He slash burns sometimes and driving by it looks like he microwaved parts of the trees just for basket makers. It's best to get a permit to gather first when in a national forest. There are times when a tree falls or loggers leave the tops after harvesting the wood. Depending on how long the trees have been down, they may be brown on top where the sun shines and green underneath. This allows for a variegated look in baskets or on top of a gourd. If the tree fell recently, the needles will still be grass green and need to dry individually first before bundling or coiling them. Dry them out of the sun in thin layers on a screen to retain their beautiful mint color. They should be turned once in a while to prevent molding, if you live in the South. Combined with sun baked chocolate brown, long leaf needles have great effects and can remain in your basket for a long time. Green needles eventually turn brown over the years unless the basket is lidded, then the inside stays green. Needles from different soil areas or some shorter needles that die with the tree itself are sometimes reddish in color. Even though they are short, they are worth using for the effect. Ponderosa needles are very short in comparison and are a light brown or beige. Their aroma bakes into each needle, if you are fortunate to find them in the eastern northwest, a very large desert area."

Green long leaf pine needles.
Photograph by Kelly Hazel.

Nancy Basket told me about her version of a mask she made from pine needles. It contains information about her Cherokee heritage. The large pine needle mask is called the Uktena Warrior mask. This is how the story goes as told by Nancy Basket.

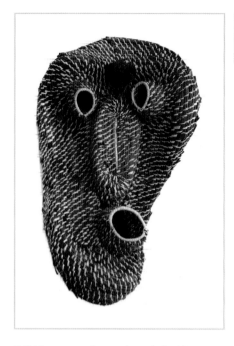

Full Uktena warrior mask made by Nancy Basket. Materials include pine needles and raffia. *Photograph by Kelly Hazel.*

Long, long time ago, when I was a little girl, I sat beside my Cherokee grandmother and listened to the stories about her side of the family in Oklahoma. I always asked questions about dad's side of the family. Sometimes I got in trouble for that. Grandma Ora was born in "Indian Territory" before it became Oklahoma. She married my grandfather when he came to her house on a horse and had another one saddled for her. When the ground dried up, and it was too hard to farm anymore, they moved to a place that had water, Washington. I was born in the Yakima Valley, surrounded by the Cascade Mountains. Grandma never knew the traditional old stories to tell me. Her life was too hard growing up in Kingston, Arkansas, to remember much from her mother, Florence Lily Fowler. This was the grandma whose grandma was Margaret Basket, who was born in Virginia. I always loved familiar stories on both sides of the fence. Grandma Ora crossed-over in a car accident when I was in the sixth grade, but I will always remember what I learned from her. My desire to know where I came from called me to the South. I grew up, married, moved to Canada and had children. Then I came back to learn pine needle basketry from a friend, Judy Arledge. I knew it was something I would do for the rest of my life. I met a Cherokee man in Union Gap who had his family's collection of pine needle baskets in the back of his bead store. I asked to buy his pine needle bear effigy basket and the cradle board. He said, "Your job isn't to buy these baskets; your job is to make them." After making baskets for a year with very short West Coast needles, I helped start the first basketry guild in the United States in modern times. The Vi Phillips/Northwest Basket Weavers Guild was formed in 1981.

When I had children, I vowed to end the unknowing, and in 1989 I moved closer to my ancestral homeland in the Carolinas to learn the Cherokee stories of respect. My children heard the stories because they were important to me, and now my grandchildren hear them too. Sometimes the stories were written in a book with no pictures, so I made pictures from leaves called kudzu. No one wants the kudzu anyway. Life is not a romantic version of what we would like it to be or what we see on TV. Not all of us learn the "old ways," not all of us know the stories. However, some of us are destined to find out anyway and pass the messages down to our own and others wanting to know. I wasn't raised on the "Rez." I know what path I've always been on. I knew how to connect the physical

Detail of Uktena warrior mask showing eyes and snake coming from the forehead. *Courtesy of Nancy Basket. Photograph by Kelly Hazel.*

events in my life with the spiritual principals I believe in, and that brought me to where I am now.

There are different versions written about the Uktena. Many include bits of other Cherokee stories and outside assumption that are not in our originals. These remain unpublished on purpose as they would eventually also be distorted. The original gist is this: Once, our people captured a Shawano warrior. In order to save his life, he offers to kill the Uktena, a giant serpent with Elk antlers, a crystal in its head, wings, and seven rings around his neck. The Uktena was always so angry he could kill your family for finding him. The warrior, who had no family but certain protections from this beast, ends up shooting the Uktena with an arrow in the 7th spot under his neck. But a drop of the poisonous blood hits the warrior between his eyes and that blood grows into a small snake. The Shawano warrior goes back to the Cherokee town and wants to live with them. They don't say a word about the snake in his head but make him live outside of town. Yet, the People come to him for healing with the crystal recovered from the serpent's head. We all have monsters in our lives. Fortunate and strong are the ones who overcome them and walk on. Many battle the demons of addiction and are never near a war. In my day my friends faced Viet Nam—some came back, but were never the same.

They were twisted like the mask. My mask honors those who fight for us. May we all remember how to treat our veterans when they return.

My baskets come from the pine needles I gather in the forests. They are sewn together, coiled from ancient stories combined with my life experiences. The Warrior was a reaction to events I couldn't change. The techniques are a part of what has anciently been preserved or found in the Cherokee culture, in memory only. Fibers deteriorate quickly in southern humidity and are less valued as archeological proofs than things more solid like stone points. Native people have a long history of borrowing, sharing, and trading with other nations. As we intermarried we brought part of where we lived and what we knew with us. We all made do with what we had growing in our back yards. Some of us are doing that today. My friend on the Qualla Boundary (known as the Cherokee reservation) says, "Even tradition has its first day on the job." If an art form is good, it will last and perhaps be preserved for others to imitate. Our Native stories are not myths, made up explanations for children. They are passed down, passed on in emerging new forms, hopefully to help history be remembered, parts never to be repeated. Thus, my representation of the Uktena Warrior mask.

Lightning Table by Nancy Basket. She made this pine needle table from a piece of wood that was hit by lightning. *Photograph by Kelly Hazel.*

Nancy Basket has created many beautiful pine needle baskets. She uses raffia to stitch the coils together. Sometimes she dyes the raffia black. The tray shown here is one of her coiled baskets. Nancy gave this description of the Lightning Tray. "The center is made from lightning-struck oak wood beside my house. Wood from a tree that is struck this way and lives is very powerful and used in some ceremonies. The lightning designs represent the four directions and all the help our West Wind Messenger has brought me during my lifetime. It is a family design that was given to me in a series of dreams, when I first moved here in 1989." The traditions have been passed down to Nancy's children and grandchildren. They have formed a non-profit organization, Native Tradition. Nancy started the kudzu leaf art cards, with the Cherokee stories on the back that began the telling of those legends and basketry abilities being shared with so many others.

Nancy Basket's daughter, Jo, made this pine needle basket. The graduating sheath made a design in the basket. *Photograph by Kelly Hazel.*

Other Varieties of Pine Needles

Peggy Wiedemann of Huntington Beach, California, uses pine needles from the Montezuma and canary pine trees. In Huntington Beach, canary pine is used in park strips, median strips, and as a landscape element. The Montezuma pine is found more in Mexico but grows in California as well. Larger pines are found there, but are not very widely used in landscaping as they are too big, too messy, and not very attractive. The following is how Peggy collects and uses her pine needles. "The natural material I use the most is pine needles, usually from Montezuma and canary pine trees. The first thing I do is collect the pine needles. Of course, I have my favorite places where I can find the needles already dry. As I collect them, I sort through them eliminating any needles that are broken, irregular or damaged. If I don't find them dry, I'll take the green needles and put them outside to slowly dry to a golden brown color. I bring the dry needles home and the first thing I do is soak them in dish soap and water for about three hours. This does two things. First, it cleans the pine needles. Second, and very importantly, it drowns any bugs or insects hiding between the needles. After they have soaked, I rinse them off several times and place them on drying racks to dry. I again sort through the needles and get rid of any that are not of good quality. The needles then dry for several days inside to ensure they will not get dirty or contaminated. I turn them several times a day until they are completely dry to avoid mold and being ruined. After I am sure they are thoroughly dry, I store them in clean basket boxes. It is important for the needles to be able to get fresh air. Storing them in plastic or any other air tight box would again seal in moisture and cause them to mold."

Peggy also shared how she uses the pine needles. "When I am ready to start weaving a basket, I take a bundle of pine needles out of my storage box. I remove the shaft that holds the individual needles together in a bundle and place them on my work table, eliminating any needles that are damaged. Then I bundle the needles in a cloth towel and tie the towel closed at the bottom, so they won't go every which way. It's better to work on my basket and not chase pine needles all day. The weaving technique I use is coiling. I add pine needles one at a time to a bundle that usually contains about thirty needles, wind this coil of pine needles in circles, and stitch them together with another natural material-waxed linen thread. So basically, I am building my basket row by row, one row at a time, each row on top of the previous row. It is a slow process, but very stimulating because each new row adds to the design and shapes the finished piece."

Detail of *In Celebration of Twirling* by Peggy Wiedemann. Coiled with pine needles and waxed linen thread. *Photography by Jan Seeger.*

Ponderosa pine needles that Nancy Basket harvested in California. *Photograph by Kelly Hazel.*

Long leaf pine needles that Nancy Basket harvested in South Carolina. *Photograph by Kelly Hazel.*

Detail of *Waves* by Peggy Wiedemann. She adds pine needles one at a time to a bundle that usually contains about thirty needles, and winds this coil of pine needles in circles and stitches them together with waxed linen thread. She builds her baskets row by row, one row at a time, each row on top of the previous row. *Photography by Jan Seeger.*

Long leaf pine needles by Barb Nelson. She runs Florida Pine Needles and her information is at the end of the book in the suppliers list. *Courtesy of Barb Nelson. Photograph by Kelly Hazel.*

Dyeing Pine Needles

There are several ways of dyeing pine needles, and many different dyes that can be used, such as RIT ®. dye and leather dye. Following you will find several ways and dyes that can be used.

Charlotte Durrence is an experienced pine needle coiler. When I need pine needles, I go to her house where she has a yard full of wonderful long leaf pine needles. Charlotte describes her technique for dyeing her pine needles.

"I have been blessed to live in an area where there are many long needle pine trees. When I started decorating gourds, I quickly realized that it would be convenient to use the pine needles to make the rims. Family and friends loved the look of the unique rims. My destiny was set. We had several pine trees in our yard and we had to clean up the needles in order to cut the grass. Thus began the journey to learn to dye the needles to compliment any type of decorated gourd."

This is the technique Charlotte uses to dye her pine needles: "I am sure there are other ways that work just as well. Pick up and sort the needles with all caps together. Be sure that each needle has a set of three blades and that the cap is intact. This is a time-consuming task, but is very important. I dye two pounds of loose needles in each batch. I have a 12" x 24" stainless steel pan that is six inches deep. I fill it with three gallons of water and heat it to almost boiling on a two-burner electric cook top. I add two bottles of Rit Fabric Dye to the water. Then, add the two pounds of pine needles to the pan. Turn the burner to medium and cook for about two hours. You may have to add a little water during the cooking time. When dyeing the needles black, I usually cook them for four hours. It is best if you leave the needles in the water overnight. The following day, I take the needles out of the dye and rinse them several times. You may add a little vinegar to the last rinse water to set the dye. At this time, it is very important to spread the needles out to dry. An old window screen works great for me. Be sure they are spread out in a thin layer. Turn them several times each day until they are completely dry. If you bundle them with rubber bands before they are dry, you will get mildew (black spots) on them. A few tips: You can use one bottle of dye to get lighter colors. It will always take two bottles for dyeing the needles black. I use a wooden spoon to turn the needles while they are cooking. It is best if this can be done outside, as a spill will be a disaster inside of the house. Keep rubber gloves handy for rinsing and spreading the needles."

I am a member of the Pine Needles Group and the Naturals Group. These are Yahoo® Groups and you can join online. Leigh Adams gave me permission to use the following information about using leather dyes. "I have used leather dyes very successfully for many years. The trick is to use boiling water to 'open up' the pine needles, and then add leather dye until you achieve the color you want. For intense colors, you may need to let the needles sit for longer periods of time. When they've reached a satisfactory color, rinse in cold water until water runs clear, and then do a vinegar/water rinse to set the color. Greens and blues are 'fugitive colors' and tend to fade out. Experiment and let people know what you learn."

Lynn Hoyt is also on the Pine Needles Group and gave this information about using RIT® dyes. "I usually do mine in the kitchen, wear plastic gloves, spread out a plastic trash bag on the counter, and put several layers of newspapers on top, and then some paper towels. I bring a gallon of water to a boil and stir in the dye until it's dissolved. You want to concentrate the color as much as you can, so don't add too much water. I use a dedicated wooden spoon with a long handle. Then I add the needles, simmer, and turn the needles until they are as dark as I like. Keep in mind that the wet needles always look darker than when they dry. Take the needles out of the dye. They'll be drippy, so put them on an old towel or thick newspapers and paper towels and go to the sink. Rinse the needles until the water runs clear. Spread them out on your absorbent papers and turn occasionally until they are completely dry."

Here is a glycerin pine needles recipe from Pam Talsky of the Pine Needles Group. Pam shared this with the group and allowed me to include it here.

Supplies:

One pound pine needles, two pints glycerin, water to cover.

Equipment:

Large roaster that fits your oven—I buy the large aluminum ones at Sam's Club® used for food service and double them for extra strength, large tongs or something to turn the needles while in the hot bath, plates to hold the needles in the bath, heavy duty rubber gloves—like the thick insulated orange ones Royalwood® sells.

Procedure:

In the roaster—pour the two pints of glycerin and add the pine needles. I split the bundle in half and put the cell ends out with the tips overlapping slightly. Add enough water to cover the pine needles. Swish the mixture around a bit to help mix the glycerin and water. Place the plates on each bundle of pine needles to keep them in the water and avoid having them burn in the oven. Turn your oven up to 250 degrees. Check in about an hour to see how they are doing. You want a nice slow simmer. If it is going too strong, reduce the temperature to 225 or 200. Allow to simmer for another hour. Check the pine needles again—while wearing your gloves! This time, remove the plates and flip the needles around to see they are getting even heat and glycerin. They should be about the same color through the whole bunch. If not, stir them up, replace the plates and leave them for one more hour in your oven. When they are done, shut the oven off and allow them to soak overnight in the solution—as they will pick up more glycerin as they cool and it is MUCH SAFER removing the needles from the batch when they are cool. I pull them out and into a bucket. Then rinse them very well with cool water, until it runs clear. Lay them out thinly on towels in an area with good air flow and allow them to dry. (I am fortunate to have tables with wire racks below that I spread the needles on—and then turn on my ceiling fans for good air flow!) Drying can take up to a week or two, depending on the humidity. If you bundle them before the water is gone, they will mold. Because of the glycerin, they may still SEEM wet! If you wish to dye the needles, add two to three packages of RIT to the glycerin and some water BEFORE you add the pine needles. Be sure to stir it up well after you add the water. It may take a bit longer to get the color you desire."

Charlotte Durrence sorting the pine needles she collected in her yard. *Photography by Derral Durrence.*

Charlotte lets the pine needles completely dry before storing so they will not mold. *Photography by Derral Durrence.*

Charlotte dyes her own pine needles with Rit® fabric dye. *Photography by Derral Durrence.*

Pine needle basket by Charlotte Durrence. She used the pine needles that she dyed black. *Photography by Derral Durrence.*

1.10: Willow

Willow, salix spp., is easy to grow and can adapt to just about any climate. Wild willow grows in a grove or thicket as shrub-like bushes. It grows from three to eight feet tall. Ditch willow is a nickname for ones growing along the roadside. The leaves are long and silvery underneath. The rods (branches) are harvested in the fall or after the first frost. Just make sure you cut them before the sap starts rising. Cut long slender rods with no branches about the size around of a pencil. Tie in a bundle to carry home. Strip the leaves off and sort by lengths. Store bundled upright in a shed or garage where the air circulates. Willow has long been used as a basketry material in many cultures. Willows must be soaked in cold water in order to make them pliable. After soaking, they should be covered in a cool spot to mellow overnight. You can learn more from Bonnie Gale, a professional willow basket maker. Bonnie's website offers imported European basketry willows, willow basketry books, and tools. Her website: www.englishbasketrywillows.com is also listed in the Suppliers Section.

Maxine Riley, a good friend and member of the Upper South Carolina Basket Makers' Guild, took a trip to Ireland. There she learned how to weave a Duck Nesting basket from willow under the direction of a local couple. Maxine said, "It is one of the most unusual baskets I have ever woven. The stick ends are stuck into the banks of the pond and the basket is then used for a nest. What a wonderful experience weaving with willow."

Duck Nesting Basket by Maxine Riley. The basket was woven with willow from Ireland. *Photograph by Kelly Hazel.*

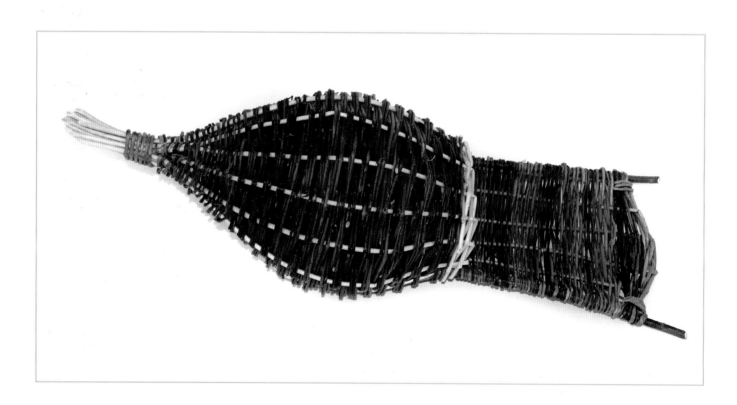

1.11: Bull Whip Kelp

Natural materials for weaving and coiling can be found just about anywhere, even in odd places. The ocean is not a place most people would think to look for weaving and coiling materials, but, sure enough, there are artist who harvest their materials from the ocean. Donna Crispin is an artist who uses bull whip kelp for one of her weaving materials.

"Many years ago, I lived near the Oregon coast. I looked forward to the winter storms, with their blustery winds and torrential rain, because they delivered basket weaving treasures for me. On my beach walk the next day, I would find two to three feet high piles of tangled up bull whip kelp, *Nereocystis luetkeana*. I'd take my snippers, cut lengths up to fifteen feet long, and then coil them up like a rope. When you are collecting, you'll want to pick pieces that are in good condition. This means that they are not soft, moldy, or battered up too much. Your kelp can be dried by putting it near a heat source, such as a wood stove, for several days. Turn it over several times, so that all sides get dry. When it is hard and inflexible, you can store it in an open box for as long as you like. The smell will dissipate as it dries. If it gets exposed to excess humidity, it softens up. In that case, you can just put it back by the heat source for awhile. You can weave with your dried kelp by throwing it in a bucket of hot water. How much time you soak it will depend on the size of your pieces. The smaller

diameter pieces should be in the water less time. Leave them in the bucket until they are flexible. If you forget about them, they will absorb too much water and there is a tremendous amount of shrinkage. You can also weave with kelp fresh off of the beach. Just remember that with any kelp basket, the moisture loss generally causes your basket to have a more open look. Kelp makes great twined and looped baskets. If you make a basket around a mold, like a can, or a glass jar, you'll have a nice, straight shape. If you don't use a mold, nature will take its course. The drying process and the varied thicknesses of the pieces you selected cause the baskets to take on a more organic look. If you have large pieces, you can sew them up like leather. They make lovely pouches, embellished with shells and ocean plants. Traditionally, bull whip kelp was a valuable resource for the coastal Native Americans from northern California to southeast Alaska. It was dried and cured, spliced and plaited. Nets, ropes, anchor lines, and harpoon lines were made of bull whip kelp. The stem and leaves are edible. If you do a little research, you can find recipes for pickled bull whip kelp."

The Pine Needles Group I belong to online has basket exchanges at times. I participated in several exchanges and in one I received a wonderful basket from Gerri Swanson. She made the basket with palm stems and wove the top rim with bull whip kelp. She lives in California on Monterey Beach, and she sent me information about collecting and preparing bull whip kelp.

Bull whip kelp basket by Gerri (Gairaud) Swanson. *Courtesy of Gerri Swanson.*

Palm stem coiled basket with bull whip kelp rim by Gerri (Gairaud) Swanson. *Courtesy of Gerri Swanson.*

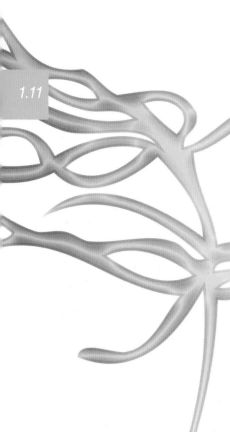

Bull whip kelp grows on exposed, rocky shores along the West Coast, from southern California up into Alaska. It is found on beaches after it has died and been tossed up on the shore from storm driven waves. It is one of the fastest growing of all the kelps; growing up to 6" in a day and up to 130' overall. It is these great lengths that make such wonderful weavers. When left on the beach, it takes months to rot, and when collected, cleaned, and dried properly, it can be used to make unique and individual creations and baskets. When collecting kelp, look for pieces that have been on the beach for awhile and are mostly dry. Sometimes, the entire holdfast (root system), stipe (stalk), and bulb can all be used. Other times, only part of the stipe might be usable or just the bulb end. Cut off any pieces that are undesirable. Remember to please leave the discarded pieces on the beach. Long thin sections make excellent weavers, while the fatter/wider parts make good spokes, especially with the attached bulb—although, both can be used in either fashion.

Using gloved hands, scrape off the sand and roll it up like a rope, starting with the thinner/holdfast end. Smaller sections can be draped over your arm, while longer, heavier bulb-ends can be dragged behind. Using raffia or a light twine, tie the bundles at two places to keep them manageable. Once home, the kelp must be washed to remove the remaining sand, salt, and algae. Use a scrubber, or the scrubber side of a kitchen sponge. An outdoor shower, a hose with a jet sprayer, or a big, plastic bucket or garbage can filled with water, are all good ways to wash kelp. Due to the amount of sand and other clinging sea particles, it's not a good idea to do the cleaning in your shower or tub. Clean the kelp as best you can, because, the cleaner it is, the less chance it has of smelling later on. Re-roll the ropes and loosely tie them up again for manageability. Shorter, flatter pieces can be doubled over and loosely tied or just hung up to dry. Hang the rolls of kelp someplace warm and dry with good air circulation. Hang them on an expandable wooden laundry dryer, over a rod in the bath, or outside on the deck rail when it's warm to dry out. The less overlapping of pieces, the faster the kelp will dry.

The kelp does have an odor while drying that many people find offensive. Outside in a sunny area, or a garage, is best to keep everyone happy (good luck with that)! It is important to let the kelp dry completely before storing it or even weaving it, otherwise it will mold. Often while drying, salt may leach out. This is not something to worry about, because it is the nature of the material. When it comes time to weave, the kelp must, once again, be washed and soaked. This final washing allows you to remove any salt that has leached out or any stray pieces of algae that weren't caught before. Soak only as long as it takes for the pieces to become pliable enough to work with. Scrubbing one last time with the scrubber also assists in unlinking the bends in the stipe that occurred during storage and decreasing the amount of time needed for soaking.

Once your kelp is pliable, you are ready to work your magic with it, or at least have fun playing with it! When your basket or other creation is complete, it will need to dry completely. This can take up to several days. It needs to have good air circulation on all sides, including and especially the bottom. Setting it on a wire cooling rack in the sun, in front of a fire, or in a warm, dry room with a circulating fan or a sunny window is a good way to accomplish the drying. It also helps to turn the item several times into the direction of the heat or fan source to insure even drying in all areas. Working with kelp in the summer, rather than in a cold, wet winter, is also a good idea. As the basket or other creation dries, it will shrink and can fold its top edges in on itself. Use a "mold" to keep it open. A glass measuring cup or bowl, or a plastic container or anything that fits inside the top edge can be used. Do not push your basket in all the way to the bottom because it could become stuck if the top shrinks down too much. Set the container just inside the top so that it can easily be removed when the kelp has dried. Kelp dries very hard and the smaller, thinner pieces can be brittle and easy to break. Bull whip kelp is an incredibly fascinating medium to work with. Its colors have such a wide, diverse spectrum, from sun-bleached white, to tans, yellows, oranges, rusts, browns of all shades, and even deep black. The textures are also numerous, some pieces being somewhat flat and smooth, while other lengths have been beaten by the surf, giving the look of a twisted rope. There are a myriad of possibilities for creativity using bull whip kelp. When other kelps are included, such as feather boa kelp, giant and split kelp, along with other sea plants and algae, shells and rocks found along the shore, there seems no limitations to the art one can create from the gifts of the sea.

1.12: Other Natural Materials

There are other natural materials that weavers use for their creations. Pamela Zimmerman uses various types of materials. Pamela describes using hardwood tree roots: "I wanted to simulate roots, but instead I decided to use real ones. I went to the old compost pile that has not been turned in years. The dirt was pretty soft and I just dug into it, rendering hair-like roots from the surrounding trees. I used them without preparation, preserving as much of the dirt as possible, to twine roots for my piece, *Uprooted.*"

Several other natural materials are grass seed heads, and chinaberry pits. Pamela Zimmerman has also used these naturals in her art. "Grass seed heads are collected while the grasses are flowering, or after the flowering, when the seeds have been disbursed by the wind. This is the seed head of the *miscanthus*, a decorative grass that grows in clumps. Simply cut from the plant and use dry in short stems; it is not very flexible. It comes in curly and straight varieties, and is seen in my piece, *Trade Cargo: Passages.* Chinaberry pits are taken from chinaberry trees. The fruit is hard and green. The flesh must be rotted off, and then the resultant mess is boiled and rubbed, and laid out in the sun to dry. The pits have a naturally soft area that can be drilled for a hole. They can be seen in my work, *Trade Cargo: Passage.*"

Hibiscus fiber is wonderful for basketry, coiling, and twining cordage. The fibers are soft and flexible and can be used natural, bleached, or dyed. Pamela Zimmerman uses this natural in her art. "Hibiscus fiber is peeled from the outside stem of the dried hibiscus plant after it dies back for the winter. It may be bleached, dyed, or used as-is. It is used in my piece *Incubation.*"

Another material that can be used for weaving is Red Osier Dogwood, *Cornus sericea.* It has bright burgundy-red bark and has been used by basket makers because of the color. It grows in the northern regions in swampy areas. You need to cut the branches in late fall or winter when the sap is not rising. The branches that are at least a year old can be used. After cutting the branches, bind them together to carry. The branches can be used for a few weeks without soaking them. Store them in a dark area so they will not dry out. When you are ready to weave, soak until they are pliable. You can use red osier branches the same way willow is used to make baskets. Angie Wagner made a basket of three species of willow and red osier dogwood grown on her farm. The orange is smoked vine rattan and the white is natural vine rattan (imported but no longer commercially available). The initial two hoops (rings) were made from the willow and red osier dogwood. Then she wove with the two vine rattans and added more willow and dogwood to the body of the basket.

Nancy Basket uses weeping willow branches and weeping birch twigs for weaving. Nancy states, "thin flowing branches can be trimmed from your trees so mowing underneath them can be accomplished easier. They coil well on gourds." Thin or split willow rods can be woven into wicker, which has a long history of basket weaving. The relatively pliable willow is less likely to split while being woven than many other woods, and can be bent around sharp corners in basketry.

Detail of *Trade Cargo Passages* by Pamela Zimmerman. *Photography by Ronald L. Sowers Photography.*

Incubation by Pamela Zimmerman. *Photography by Ronald L. Sowers Photography.*

A basket made by Angie Wagner. She used willow, red osier dogwood, and vine rattan. *Courtesy of Angie Wagner.*

Dyed coir. *Photograph by Kelly Hazel.*

Gourd Universe by Terri Schmit. Materials include devil's claw painted red, goldenrod gall painted black, and wire. *Courtesy of Terri Schmit.*

Coir is a natural fiber that can be used in coiling and weaving. It is the fibrous material found between the hard, internal shell and the outer coat of a coconut. It is in rope form when you get it from a supplier, and it can be dyed very vibrant colors. It can be a little hard on your hands as you weave and because of the size of the rope, you would use it in a large basket or as a rim on a gourd. You can take the individual fibers and use them to weave with in smaller baskets.

Terri Schmit lives on a farm in Wisconsin and loves to hike. On her hikes, she gathers natural materials to incorporate into her art. One item she particularly looks for is golden gall. "This is a gall or almost a perfectly round ball which is an imperfection in the goldenrod plant as a result of a particular wasp which lays its eggs in the flower's stem. The stems are quite strong and can be used on gourds. Collect the stems in the spring after they've dried out all winter. Wipe them clean and then you can use them in their natural state or you can paint them. Shelf fungus is another natural Terri uses. "The shelf fungus can usually be found growing near the base of oak trees. You can pick them right off the tree and then leave them out to dry. After they have dried out (this may take a month) place them in a sealed bag and put them in the freezer to make sure any bugs are eliminated. You can also dip them in a bleach/water solution. I use them just as they are, usually as a base for spirit dolls or even small vases and bowls. Some shelf fungi are quite large and can really add something special to a piece. Once they're dry, they're quite hard."

Many gourd and pine needle artists use walnuts. Walnuts can be sliced and used for starts for a pine needle basket or for decoration on baskets and gourds. Terri Schmit uses walnut petioles in her gourd art. "We have an abundance of black walnut trees on our property. In the fall, when the leaves fall, the petioles are left on the ground (these are the stems to which the leaves are connected). Some petioles can be over twelve inches long. I will collect handfuls of these on my daily walks. I remove any leafy material that might still be on the petioles, usually near the tips, then rinse them in water and leave them to dry. I keep them stored in a plastic container and they'll last forever. When you're ready to use them, they need to be soaked in water for about thirty minutes until they become pliable. Petioles are very similar to pine needles in that they have a knobby end. I never remove this end because I love the texture it provides. However, you can clip it off, if you prefer. Because the petioles are thicker at the bottom than near the tip, you can't calibrate the width of your coil as easily as when you use pine needles. I usually start with a few in my coil and add as I need to. Petioles can be dyed using a regular wood and reed dye."

One more natural material is Job's tears. This plant goes by various names, including David's tears, Saint Mary's tears, Christ's tears, and just plain tear drops. Job's tears have been used for making shaker gourds, probably one of the earliest musical instruments. In Africa, hollow gourds are covered with a loose net strung with hundreds of Job's tears. As the beads slap against the gourd, a loud shaker sound is produced. Using the neck of the gourd as a handle, the sound of the bead net is amplified by the hollow gourd. Terri Schmit has been growing Job's tears in Wisconsin. "I have grown Job's tears here in Wisconsin. Usually, Job's tears grow in Hawaii or very warm climes, but one year I planted five seeds and got five huge plants and hundreds of Job's tears. They are nature's plant and produce a small grayish bead which has a natural hole through it, ready to be strung and, of course, added to a gourd!"

Some gourd artists in the southwestern part of the United States use cholla cactus wood. Sandra Phillips sent me photographs of the wood. Cholla cactus represents more than twenty species of the *Opuntia* genus, family *cactaceae*. Cholla is a term applied to various shrubby cacti of this genus with cylindrical stems composed of segmented joints. It has bark and large needles. Cholla cactus are found in the hot deserts of the American southwest, with different species having adapted to different locale and elevation ranges. Like most cactus, cholla have tubercles, which are small, wart-like projections on the stems, from which sharp spines, actually modified leaves, grow. But cholla is the only cactus with papery sheaths that cover their spines. Maggie LeDuc from Cypress, California, told me that when the cholla cactus dies you can scrape the needles and skin off the wood. That makes it smooth and the wood is hard. The holes are left where the tubercles were located. It is an interesting natural to add to a gourd or as a stand for a basket. Prickly pear cactus is also a member of the opuntia genus, but their branches are pads rather than cylindrical joints. Judy Richie uses cactus fiber in her gourds. She uses the dried skeleton found in the pad of the prickly pear cactus. She said, "Go out and find prickly pear cactus pads that have fallen from the plant and dried. Carefully, remove the dried skin, wearing gloves. Then, wash the dried skeleton fiber with Clorox® and soap. With a strong spray of water, attempt to clean out any dried membrane."

Walnut slices attached to a bark berry basket. *Photograph by Kelly Hazel.*

Dried cholla cactus wood with bark removed. *Courtesy of Sandra Phillips.*

Crazy Gourd by Judy Richie. She used the skeleton of a prickly pear cactus for this texture. The cactus was glued in a carved area. *Courtesy of Judy Richie.*

Man-Made Materials

The materials for weaving or coiling that are manmade are endless. I was looking through the book, *500 Baskets*, by Lark Books, and found the following materials that were used in some exquisite baskets: copper electrical wire, cotton archival paper, metallic thread, satin ribbon, sheet metal, glass beads, upholstery tacks, synthetic gold leaf, a goat skull, tape measures, and the list could go on. Experimenting with some extraordinary materials can be so much fun! Use your imagination! Below I will go into a little more detail with materials that either I or my friends have used.

Close up of Laraine Short's woven gourd. The rim is a six ply wax cord and wire. She added a little interest to the design with beads. *Photograph by Kelly Hazel.*

1.13: Cloth

Who would think that cloth could be used for weaving, but it can. You can use a favorite fabric to coil a basket or on top of gourds. My friend, Becky Folsom, showed me how to use cloth and place it over a core and coil on top of a gourd. She calls her technique "Ragtops." To begin a ragtop, cut the end of the cloth at an angle and start wrapping around a core (I use welt cord made of cotton used in making welt in upholstery). You will need to drill holes around the gourd about 1/4" from the top and 1/2" apart. The coils are then stitched to the gourd and together with thread or wax linen thread to form the top of a gourd. How many rows you stitch are determined by the size of the gourd you have. You can also use strips of cloth to weave in a rib basket. Claudette Hart uses cloth in a different way, "I've taken rag rugs apart and used the strands, which I dyed." Marla Helton recycles old sweaters by cutting them into strips to use in her weaving. She does the weaving on a piece of pottery or a gourd.

Pottery vase with fibers, sweaters, seagrass, dyed baling twine, and reed. Made by Marla Helton. *Photography by Stuart A. Fabe.*

Plastic craft cording, also called gimp or boondoggle or lanyard. It is a plastic lacing used to make bracelets, key chains, and bookmarks. *Photography by Kelly Hazel.*

1.14: Cords, Threads, Yarns, Fibers, and Others

There are so many cords, threads, and yarns that can be woven into your weaving and coiling. When I make undulating gourds, I use mohair and other interesting yarns as a part of the weaving. You can find a pattern for one of these baskets in my first book, *Weaving on Gourds*. The yarns create texture and color to the woven gourd. Also found in the first book is a gourd by Susan Byra. Susan used fun fur and eyelash yarn as part of coiling on a gourd. She is also planning a gourd creation using the little eyelets used in scrap booking, along with different shapes punched from aluminum drink cans. Joyce Laverty uses special ribbons. "I have recently ordered and received sari silk ribbons and yarns from Nicole at darngoodyarns.com. These yarns are up-cycled yarns, created by women in India and Nepal by collecting remnants of sari silk fabric. Our purchases help Indian and Nepali women provide basic needs for themselves as well as their children. The silks are beautiful—the colors striking. I have only had time to use them once." Barb Nelson uses ladder yarns. "I love using the 'ladder' yarns (a novelty yarn) to coil pine needles, particularly the copper colored ones. The color stands out nicely on natural needles without being too overstated. You can purchase the yarn at any yarn or craft shop." Donna Crispin uses silk fibers in her baskets. You can order silk fibers and mulberry fibers online. Waxed linen thread is used to make baskets and for the stitching material for coiling. Just consider all the cords they make now. I have some colorful plastic cording I used to teach the children to braid on a Kumihimo loom in vacation Bible school. I plan on using that cord to weave on top of a gourd. It is flexible and can be used just like round reed to twine.

Waxed linen thread. *Photography by Kelly Hazel.*

Black and white horsehair. *Photography by Kelly Hazel.*

Gourd Basket by Donna Sakamoto Crispin. Materials include silk fiber, papier-mâché, western red cedar, and wire. *Courtesy of Donna Sakamoto Crispin.*

Detail of Angie Craft's coiled gourd. She used Danish cording, yarn, waxed linen thread, and beads. *Photography by Kelly Hazel.*

Pamela Zimmerman uses horsehair to weave beautiful baskets. I took a workshop given by Pamela at a basket convention. We made a basket on an acorn cap using horsehair and sinew. Horsehair can be obtained by clipping your own from underneath the horse's tail. It must be washed, dried, and placed in bags to keep it from getting tangled. Placing rubber bands around each end will help. Some suppliers carry natural and dyed horsehair. Bonnie Gibson uses horsehair in some of her masks.

According to Wikipedia®, an online free encyclopedia, "Mizuhiki is an ancient Japanese art form that uses a special cord. The cord is created from rice paper, tightly wound, starched to give it stiffness, and then colored. This art form was used to tie up the hair of the samurai." I use mizuhiki with my coiling. Lay a piece of mizuhiki along side of the cording and it brings a sparkle to the piece. Mizuhiki can also be added to woven baskets for sparkle.

One more item I will mention, used in baskets and gourds, is antlers. Betsey Sloan has just published a book through Schiffer Publishing, Ltd. titled *Antler Art for Baskets and Gourds.* It is a wonderful book for those wanting to learn how to use antlers in your baskets and gourds. My friend Judy Richie from Texas taught a class at a retreat I attended using antlers in a coiled gourd. It was a fun class and I learned how to anchor an antler in my coiling on gourds. Jill Choate, originally from Alaska, is a basket maker who uses gourds in her baskets. Judy and Jill go to many conventions, gourd shows, and retreats to teach classes. If you ever get a chance to take one of their classes, do so. You will learn a lot! When I first started weaving baskets I tried using an antler as a handle. It was a lot of fun. I purchased a shed antler from a trader company in the Southwest, figured out how to attach my spokes, and then wove a rib basket.

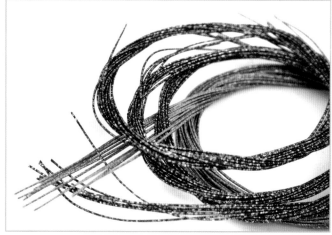

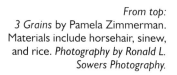

From top:
3 Grains by Pamela Zimmerman. Materials include horsehair, sinew, and rice. *Photography by Ronald L. Sowers Photography.*

Mizuhiki is a colorful Japanese paper cord and can be used in coiling and weaving to add some sparkle. *Photography by Kelly Hazel.*

Judy Richie uses antlers in her pine needle coiling. *Photography by Kelly Hazel.*

Things like feathers, pods, and many other items can be used. You can weave baskets, coil on gourds, or add embellishments with so many different natural materials. As I have said before, just look around you and see what is available or order materials from suppliers. Then get busy!

Close up of Angie Craft's coiled gourd with a peacock feather. *Photography by Kelly Hazel.*

Penny Reynolds' gourd is woven with yarns and seagrass and has chinaberry, jacaranda, and eucalyptus bell pods as embellishments. *Photography by Kelly Hazel.*

Close up of Angie Craft's coiled pine needle antler gourd with a feather added. *Photography by Kelly Hazel.*

1.15: Paper

Paper, produced from trees, is both a natural and an easily accessible material. Paper is such an unusual material for baskets and gourds that I decided to list it in this section. I taught elementary art in the public and private schools for thirty-eight years. I made paper baskets with the children because it was an inexpensive material and many times the supply budget was small. We used magazines and newspapers to make baskets. One basket utilized magazine pages cut into strips and then woven to make a small basket. The magazine pages added an element of color to the baskets. In the book, *Making Creative Baskets,* by Jane Laferla, there are several patterns for paper baskets made with poster paper, laminated paper, newspaper, and even a paper bag. Check it out for some really creative baskets.

My friend, Sandy Roback, makes paper baskets using watercolor paper. If you want to experiment with painted paper, here's your chance. In the projects section, Sandy tells you how to prepare your paper and weave your basket. She even paints beautiful scenes on the paper baskets. I have also seen baskets made with handmade paper and even ones that were dipped in wet paper pulp and dried. Becky Folsom shared that brown paper bags make good gourd rims. She said, "Wad up the paper bag, tear off any smooth edge, and twist and secure around rims with waxed linen." So your imagination can go wild when making a contemporary basket or gourd.

Sandy Roback makes baskets from watercolor paper. *Photography by Kelly Hazel.*

Sandy Roback made this paper basket and painted a watercolor scene on the front. *Photography by Kelly Hazel.*

Jackie Abrams has taken paper to a new height. She transforms simple materials into contemporary works of art. She says, "My work is a progression of explorations." Some of her baskets are woven with cotton paper and wire and are coated with several layers of encaustic wax or Ghanaian-batiked fabric and recycled glass beads. Some are coated with the "natural colors of the earth." She also makes traditional cathead baskets, woven of painted cotton paper.

Twill Baskets by Jackie Abrams. Traditional cathead baskets, woven of painted cotton paper. *Courtesy of Jackie Abrams.*

Talking Sisters by Jackie Abrams. Woven with cotton paper and wire, these sisters are coated with several layers of encaustic wax, embedded with lines and layers of conversation. *Courtesy of Jackie Abrams.*

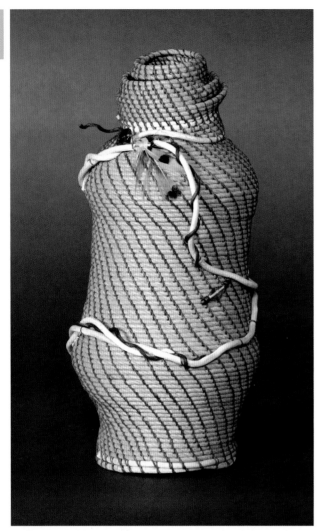

Paper cording is used for coiling baskets and on gourds. Marla Helton and Stu Fabe use Danish cording, a three ply paper cording, to create beautiful coiled gourds. Danish cording has a little different appearance than regular paper cording. Both are used for weaving chair seats. Marla uses a spray floral paint to add muted color to the Danish cording. You can order paper cording from many basket and gourd suppliers. Paper rush and even paper twist can be used for weaving and coiling.

I use white paper rush. It is white, twisted round paper cord. You can dye it, but do not allow it to soak for any length of time. I boil the water and then add the dye. I keep the paper rush coiled and dip it in the dye. Many times I space dye. I have three to four dye colors. I take one side of the coil and dip it in a color, turn the coil and dip another side in a different color. Continue this until you color the entire coil. Let the coil dry completely. I use this for coiling on top of my gourds. The paper matches the design in the gourd.

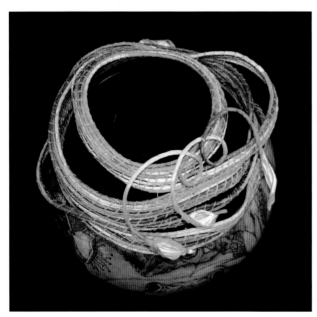

Coiled Divine by Marla Helton is woven with Danish cord. *Photography by Stuart A. Fabe.*

Frogs by the author is coiled with dyed white paper cording. *Photography by Kelly Hazel.*

Black Maria by Stuart Fabe. The sculptural gourd is coiled with Danish cord. *Photography by Stuart A. Fabe.*

1.16: Wire and Metals

Wire-coiled baskets have been created for hundreds of years out of thin wire that is woven around itself to create a useful storage container. Wire is an inexpensive material that can be used with just a few simple tools. There are elaborate baskets made with many different types of wire.

Bonnie Gibson, a master gourd artist, shared photographs of a basket and several gourds she created using copper wire in the weaving. The basket is woven with round and flat pieces of the copper wire. Bonnie attached the wire to one gourd and used the wire as spokes for her weaving.

Donna Crispin uses wire in many of her baskets. In fact, several of her baskets are made entirely of wire. Laraine Short uses wire as a rim for a gourd and hangs wire embellishments and beads from the wire rim. Marla Helton uses wire-covered bark for making baskets and gourds. This material can be ordered from suppliers.

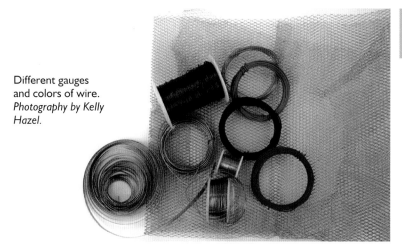

Different gauges and colors of wire. *Photography by Kelly Hazel.*

Copper Basket by Bonnie Gibson. *Courtesy of Bonnie Gibson.*

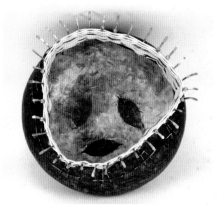

Top detail of a woven gourd by Bonnie Gibson. She used copper for spokes and wove with round read, adding beads in the design. *Courtesy of Bonnie Gibson.*

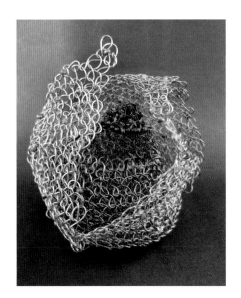

Pod Basket by Donna Sakamoto Crispin. Technique is knotless netting with copper wire and beads. *Courtesy of Donna Sakamoto Crispin.*

Laraine Short used wire as a rim for a gourd and had wire embellishments hanging from the rim. *Photography by Kelly Hazel.*

Bark Covered Wire Basket by Marla Helton. Bark covered wire, seagrass, reed. *Photography by Stuart A. Fabe.*

Debbie Wilson has used telephone wire for a gourd woven rim—very unique! Recycled wire makes for a great rim and is easily obtained from electricians and telephone/cable employees. Just be resourceful!

Wire mesh is another interesting material to utilize. Marla Helton teaches a dragonfly class using wire and tubular wire mesh. I ordered tubular wire mesh from Beaded Lily in Florence, Italy. You bend the wire to form a dragonfly shape and pull the tubular wire mesh over the wings. This mesh could be used in baskets as well.

Debbie Wilson used telephone wire on this gourd. *Photography by Kelly Hazel.*

Debbie Wilson used wire and beads on this gourd. *Photography by Kelly Hazel.*

The author made this dragonfly using wire mesh in a class by Marla Helton. *Photography by Kelly Hazel.*

1.17: Recycled and Other Materials

Other recycled materials, such as wire scraps that are to be discarded, can be found at any telephone, cable, or electric company. Sweaters, cut in strips, are a great source of recycled items. Donna Crispin uses recycled bamboo in some of her baskets. Old bamboo furniture is great to recycle. Cut the bamboo and make strips to use in weaving or for a strong material for a woven structure. Jackie Abrams uses recycled materials in her coiled baskets. She used recycled silk blouses and waxed linen thread or black plastic bags from Ghana and waxed linen thread. In Ghana, these bags are called "rubbers." In Uganda, they are called polythins, or just "polys." She talks on her web site about the women forms and coiled baskets she makes, "Using the ancient technique of coiling found almost universally in African societies, these pieces are inspired by my recent work with women in Ghana and Uganda—their spirit, their culture, and their energy in the streets. This work is evolving. I use the materials at hand and work intuitively, letting the form develop as it grows. Each coil captures the experience of the moment. The form develops a shape, stitch by stitch, coil by coil, experience by experience. These experiences are the threads of our lives that hold us together, give us form, make each of us the person we become."

Bamboo basket made by Donna Sakamoto Crispin. Materials include silk fiber, papiermâché, recycled bamboo strips, wire, and bamboo leaves. *Courtesy of Donna Sakamoto Crispin.*

The plastic bags that fruit, onions, and other items come in can also be used in weaving. They can be used as core for coiling or actually cut in strips and woven. One basket in *Making Creative Baskets* is made of plastic tubing and plastic cording. The tubes form the coils and the coils are tied together with the cord. Leftover plastic tubing makes great gauges for coiling pine needles.

The Poly Sisters by Jackie Abrams are coiled baskets using recycled materials. Coiled with black plastic bags from Ghana and waxed linen thread. In Ghana, these bags are called "rubbers." In Uganda, they are called polythins, or just "polys." *Courtesy of Jackie Abrams.*

Section Two:

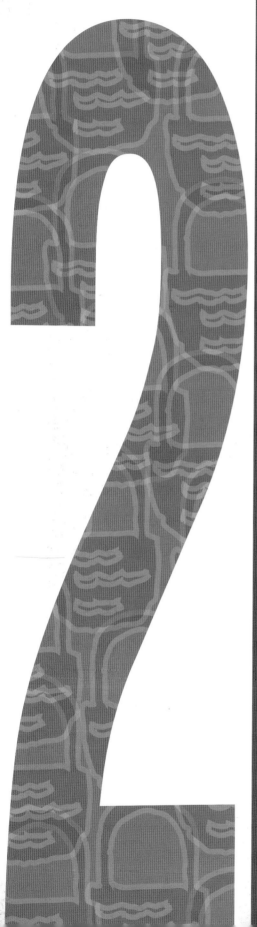

2

Projects

Baskets

Supplies Needed

- **Watercolor paper,** 18" x 24" 140lb cold pressed, 100% cotton
- **Pasta maker** (optional) with Fettuccine and/or Trenette blades
- **Acrylic paints,** 3 colors, dark, medium, and light hues
- **Brush,** 1 inch utility
- **Small water container**
- **Styrofoam tray or plate**
- **Newspaper**
- **Pencil**
- **Yardstick**
- **Scissors**
- **White glue**
- **Waxed linen thread** or a heavy thread (like buttonhole thread)
- **Large eye craft needle**
- **Small craft clothespins**

Materials used to make the paper baskets.
Courtesy of Sandra Roback.

2.1: Paper Business Card Basket

by Sandy Roback

If you've never experimented with painted paper, here's your chance. If you have made other painted paper projects, then you probably have some left over paper you could use. Here's a useful little basket that can be easily made with all those bits and pieces.

This is a beginner basket, but you must be familiar with some basic basket terms.

Basket measures 3 1/2" L x 1 3/4" W x 1 3/4" H.

Paper baskets by Sandy Roback.
Photography by Kelly Hazel.

Preparing the Paper

1. Cover the work area with newspaper and place watercolor paper on it.

2. Put small amounts of the three colors of paint onto a styrofoam plate. Apply colors in a random pattern. Allow some colors to blend but don't mix too much.

3. Work quickly and freely when applying the paint. Crisscross the strokes and don't worry about what it looks like. (The paper will be cut up so it doesn't matter.) Applying paint too thick will make it very difficult to cut or weave the paper.

4. Allow the paper to dry completely. Use a hairdryer if you want the paper to dry a little faster.

5. After the first side is completely dry, flip the paper over and paint this side using only one color. I personally like to use a metallic, it is much more interesting. You can add some brush strokes of the metallic on the first side as well.

6. Allow the paper to dry. You can use a hairdryer if you are in a hurry; otherwise let the paper dry for several hours.

Note: The paper must be absolutely dry before it is cut. If it isn't dry you will shred the paper and mess up the cutter.

Processing the Paper

The 18" x 24" sheet of watercolor paper seems like a big piece of paper for such a small project, and it is, however, you can make more than one of this little basket or create something else with the remaining paper.

1. Cut a strip of paper 5 1/4" wide by 24" long.

2. Use the Fettuccine blade to cut the paper into strips. This will give you approximately 20 strips about 1/4" wide. Use these as spokes and/or weavers.

3. If you have the Trenette blade, cut another strip 3" wide by 24" long. This will yield approximately 24 strips about 1/8" wide. Use these as weavers and/or accents.

Preparing the materials. *Courtesy of Sandra Roback.*

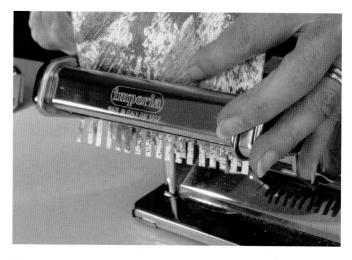

Use a pasta machine to process the paper. *Courtesy of Sandra Roback.*

Processing the paper. *Courtesy of Sandra Roback.*

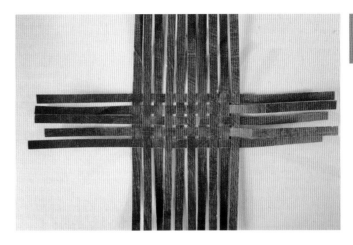

Weaving the base of the basket. *Courtesy of Sandra Roback.*

Weaving the Paper

1. Using five of the 1/4" strips cut 9 inches from each strip. Then fold and cut the remainder of the strips in half. This will yield ten pieces about 7 - 7 1/2".

2. Weave a base of five spokes by ten spokes. Be sure to leave small square spaces about 1/8". Do not pack the spokes tight.

3. The base should measure 3 1/2" x 1 3/4". Upset all spokes.

4. Begin weaving on the long sides, one row at a time alternating sides. Overlap only one spoke instead of the traditional over four. Overlapping four spokes creates too much bulk.

5. Be creative—you can use all 1/4" weavers, use all 1/8" weavers, alternate sizes, flip the weaver over to create a variety of color patterns.

6. Weave until the basket is 1 3/4" high including the rim row.

7. Cut all spokes to 1/4" and fold over the rim row inside and outside. Secure with a dot of glue, clip, and allow to dry for a few minutes.

8. Use two pieces of the 1/4" strips. Place one strip inside and one outside, overlap about 1/2".

9. Use a tapestry needle to double lash the rim with waxed linen or a heavy thread.

Step 7 of weaving the paper. Cut all spokes to 1/4" and fold over the rim row inside and outside. Secure with a dot of glue, clip, and allow to dry for a few minutes. *Courtesy of Sandra Roback.*

Finished paper basket. *Courtesy of Sandra Roback.*

2.2: Twined Wire Acorn Pendant

by Donna Sakamoto Crispin

I first learned about weaving with wire from Marilyn Moore. After weaving with reed and natural materials for many years, Marilyn introduced me to shimmering colors and sculptural possibilities. I thank her for the inspiration for this project, and her dedication as a basketry instructor. This is an Intermediate Project; twining experience necessary.

In steps 1-4 of the procedures you prepare the acorn for the project. *Courtesy of Donna Sakamoto Crispin.*

Twined Wire Acorn Pendant by Donna Sakamoto Crispin. *Courtesy of Donna Sakamoto Crispin.*

Supplies Needed
Materials:
- **An acorn** with cap
- **30 or 32 gauge wire**
- **1" #20 gauge wire**
- **Peeled spruce** or pine roots (1 foot, 2-3 mm width)
- **Super Glue®**

Tools:
- **Wire cutters**
- **Basketry shears**
- **Small rubber bands,** size 10 works
- **Another small, wider rubber band**
- **Drill**
- **Jewelry pliers**

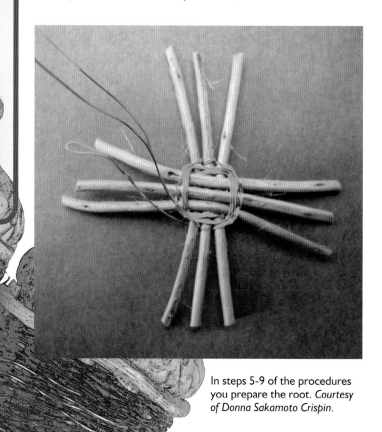

In steps 5-9 of the procedures you prepare the root. *Courtesy of Donna Sakamoto Crispin.*

Procedure:

1. Remove the cap from your acorn, and glue it back on, so that it won't come off sometime later.

2. Using a small drill bit, about the width of a medium sized needle, drill a hole in the center of the cap, straight down, about half way into the acorn.

3. Super Glue one end of the #20 wire into the hole in the acorn. Let all of the glue dry for several hours. Check part way through to make sure the glue is holding.

4. Making the loop: since everyone has different sized acorns, the lengths of your wires will vary. Adjust the length of the wire to make a small loop for your chain. On this project, with a one inch acorn, about 5/16" was left. With your round nosed jewelry pliers, bend the free end over to make a loop. Pinch the bottom of the loop with flat nose pliers, so that your chain doesn't slip out.

5. Split your root in half. When you are working with it, you'll want the rounded side out; flat side against the acorn.

6. Cut six pieces of root that is double the length of the acorn. My pieces are 2" each. Keep the remaining root in your damp towel. If you have a large acorn, you should use eight pieces.

7. Soak the roots in water for 5-10 minutes, until they are flexible. Then wrap them in an absorbent towel for 15 minutes. Leave the remaining piece for the rim in the towel.

8. Cut 2-3 weaver pieces from the 30 or 32 gauge wire, about 4 feet long.

9. Arrange your root pieces so that three are vertical. Lay the other three in the center, going horizontally.

10. Fold your weaver pieces in half, and start twining around the base, starting with the vertical bundle, and going clockwise.

11. Weave two or three rows in groups of four, then separate to single pieces of root.

In steps 10-17 of the procedures you weave the basket. *Courtesy of Donna Sakamoto Crispin.*

12. Check and see how big the base is. When it can cover the bottom, you will weave the basket on the acorn.

13. Put a dab of Super Glue on the bottom of the acorn. If you put too much on, it will show through your weaving. Put the rubber band on the outside of the basket, running vertically, from the bottom to the pendant loop. This will hold your basket to the acorn so that you get a nice, snug fit.

14. Now you need to upset the roots. Bend them up towards the cap as you are weaving. Weave right over the rubber band. If you can't get a rubber band around the acorn, try a piece of wire. If you need to stop, put a small rubber band horizontally around the acorn and the root spokes, near the cap. Spray the roots a bit before you start weaving again. Keep your roots damp, but not soaking wet.

15. Continue weaving up the sides, changing colors as you run out. Make sure loose ends are tucked behind the basket.

16. Weave up the sides until the weaving is about 1/4" from the cap. Cut the root spokes so that they are nearly touching the acorn cap.

17. Continue weaving until you are almost out of space. You might want to twine your last few rows with just a single piece of wire.

18. Find the remaining piece of root for the rim piece. Figure out the length by placing it around the very top of the nut, covering the spokes. Cut it so that the ends meet flush. Super Glue your rim piece on top of the spokes, right below the cap.

19. Put a larger rubber band on top of the rim piece, and let it dry for a few hours. (**Hint:** tie a knot in the rubber band to make it smaller.)

In steps 18-19 you finish the basket.
Courtesy of Donna Sakamoto Crispin.

Finished *Twined Wire Acorn Pendant* by Donna Sakamoto Crispin. *Courtesy of Donna Sakamoto Crispin.*

2.3: Kudzu Random Freeform Basket

by Nancy Basket

This is a beginner's basket. Carefully study the diagrams. Remember this is a free form basket, so don't be so particular about even spacing.

Kudzu Random Freeform Basket by Nancy Basket. Photography by Kelly Hazel.

Supplies Needed

Materials:

Kudzu fibers (see the chapter on kudzu to find out how Nancy processes the fibers).

Procedure

1. Tie a balloon on a stick (circle and tail). This is your base. When the kudzu gets short, tie it to the outside, anywhere. Tie on a new piece somewhere else.

2. Cross the circle with the tail.

3. Bring the tail through the circle and to the side.

4. Cross the first piece of kudzu.

5. Weave over and under each piece of kudzu until the base is covered. There is no set pattern.

6. Make small loops on the outside of the base.

7. Go through each loop on successive rounds. Fill in each loop as much as possible.

8. Push on the base as rounds are completed to make the basket. Form and shape the basket up.

9. Braid kudzu or wrap more than one kudzu length around the handle tied to each side for strength.

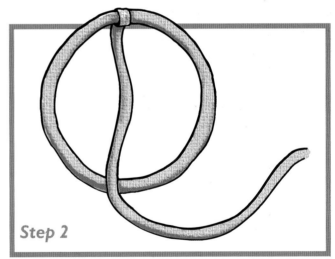

Step 2

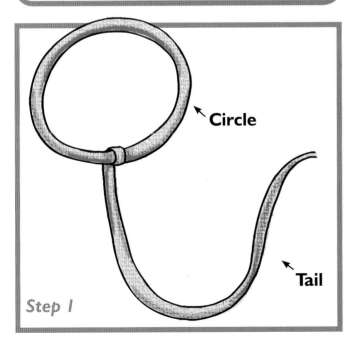

Circle

Tail

Step 1

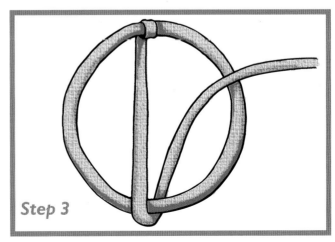

Step 3

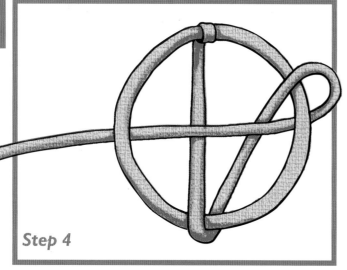

Step 4

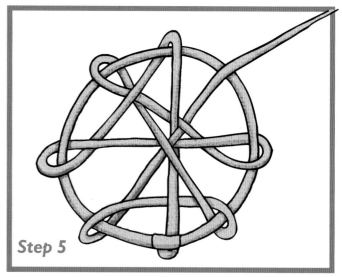

Step 5

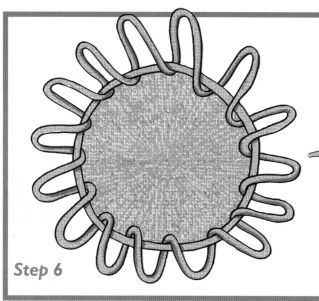

Step 6

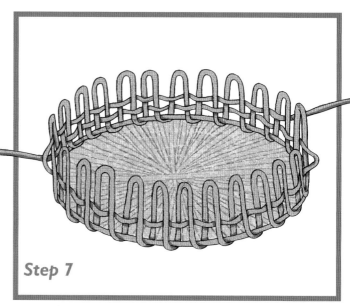

Step 7

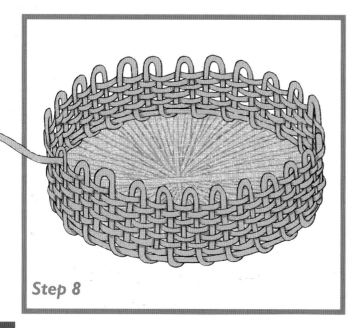

Step 8

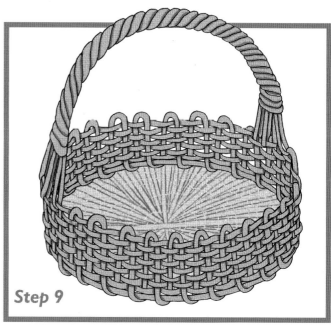

Step 9

2.4: Twill Chevron Arrow Carryall

by Pati English

This basket is an original pattern for the intermediate to advanced weaver.

Note: This Twill Weave Carryall Basket begins with an over 2 under 2 twill. Look for the pattern moving on a diagonal to the right in a "stair step" design. The Chevron Arrow accent, historically found in Native American basketry, is completed with dyed accent reed for greater contrast with base spokes split to allow an over 4 under 4 twill weave. At this time, I designed the twill with a D handle included as a spoke not yet found in print. Pattern tested by Gwen Clark.

Twill Chevron Arrow Carryall by Pati English. Photography by Kelly Hazel.

View of the twill chevron arrow. *Photography by Kelly Hazel.*

View of the inside of the handle. *Photography by Kelly Hazel.*

View of the handle. *Photography by Kelly Hazel.*

Procedure for TWILL BASE

1. Cut spokes as listed and soak until flexible.

2. Begin with 20 spokes at 40" long, mark with a pencil in the center on the rough side. Place 18 spokes at 40" on the table horizontally, marked sides up and center marks lined up. Leave very little space between spokes, then anchor with a spoke weight. Mark the inside center of the 14" x 16" "D" handle and place it horizontally (as if it were a spoke) on top of the two center horizontal spokes, spokes #9 and #10, so the spokes are under the handle. They will serve as overlay spokes. Base layout will be 8 spokes, handle, 8 spokes. To complete the twill base in an over 2 under 2 pattern using a handle, 2 overlay spokes at 40" are placed on the inside of the handle following the shape of the handle. Clip overlay spokes and handle together.

3. Weave a twill base with the 24 spokes at 36" long vertically through the original horizontal spokes.

OPTION #1: Weave the twill base starting at the left side on the inside of the handle, weaving under two spokes, over two and continue to the opposite side matching center mark. The next vertical spoke is woven to the right of the first, over one, under two, over two, etc. See chart below. When you reach the center mark on the handle, there will be 12 spokes, continue with the remaining 12 to the right of the center mark. Vertical spokes will be spaced approximately 1/8" apart, not quite touching each other. Use the inside handle overlay spokes to complete the over two, under two twill pattern, repeating the pattern every four spokes. See chart to the right.

OPTION # 2: Choose to weave the first spoke to the right of the center marks beginning under the first two spokes from the bottom of the base then over two spokes, under two, and continue weaving through to the top/opposite end. Pull until the center mark on the vertical spoke matches the center spokes, or approximately 12" - 13" past the woven base. Weave the next spoke to the right of the first and follow the chart to the right:

SPOKES ON RIGHT SIDE OF CENTER MARKS:

SPOKE #1: U2 O2 U2 O2 ...ends with U2
SPOKE #2: O1 U2 O2 U2 ...ends with U1
SPOKE #3: O2 U2 O2 U2 ...ends with O2
SPOKE #4: U1 O2 U2 O2 ...ends with O1
SPOKE #5: U2...SAME AS SPOKE #1
SPOKE #6: O1...SAME AS SPOKE #2
SPOKES #7-12 COMPLETE THE TWILL PATTERN

4. Pack these 12 spokes from the center mark to the inside of the handle, keeping minimal space between vertical spokes.

SPOKES ON LEFT SIDE OF CENTER

MARKS: These remaining 12 spokes are woven in reverse of the pattern above. Weave left of the original spokes and begin under one, over two. Pack as you go.

SPOKE #1: U1 O2 U2 O2 ...ends with O1
SPOKE #2: O2 U2 O2 U2 ...ends with O2
SPOKE #3: O1 U2 O2 U2 ...ends with U1
SPOKE #4: U2 O2 U2 O2 ...ends with U2
SPOKE #5: U1...SAME AS SPOKE #1
SPOKE #6: O2...SAME AS SPOKE #2
SPOKES #7-12: COMPLETE THE TWILL PATTERN
OVER 2 UNDER 2 TWILL WEAVE

Option: Twine 1 row with #0 or #1mm round reed in an over 2 under 2 pattern.

5. "Upsett" spokes and clothespin corners to help shape side walls of this basket. With 3/8" flat reed, begin twill weave over spokes #5 and #6 on the long side of the basket. Continue weaving to the right, under spokes #7 and #8, over the next 2, and around the basket, square off corners. Use small clips or clothespins as needed to keep weaver packed down. Overlap four spokes to end each row, then give the basket a quarter turn to the next side and weave over spokes #2 and #3, under the next 2 and continue packing each row as it is woven.

Close up of the weaving on the handle.
Photography by Kelly Hazel.

6. Weave a total of 12 rows with 3/8" flat reed in the twill pattern. Move up or over one spoke to the right of the previous row, and split the "pair" using one spoke on the right of the pair and the next spoke to the right. Check the shape of the basket and "pinch" corners to square off as the basket progresses. Keep equal spacing between vertical spokes, check to keep spokes upright and straight.

CHEVRON ARROW

7. Soak long ends of spokes until soft and flexible. Carefully split each spoke in half lengthwise down to the top row of 3/8" weavers. With 3/16" or 1/4" flat or flat oval reed, continue the over 2 under 2 twill, which now becomes over 4 under 4. Split the group of 4 spokes and use the 3 on the right side plus one additional spoke to the right, a total of 4 spokes, over these 4, then under 4. This will create a fine arrow when finished.

8. Twill weave for 8 rows. To reverse the twill and create the Chevron Arrow, begin the next weaver (row 9 of arrow) by shifting to the left one spoke. Continue to weave in the same direction, over 4, under 4 while the twill reverses to form an arrow shape for a total of 8 rows, or to the desired height.

9. Shape the sides and corners of the basket, re-wet as necessary.
   Rim Row: With #1mm round reed, twine for three rows around the top of the basket, following the over 4 under 4 pattern, or weave one row 3/8" flat reed in the over 2 under 2 pattern. Be sure spokes are standing upright.

10. **RIM:** To finish the top rim of the basket, soak the spokes that extend above the sides of the basket by turning it upside down in the sink. When flexible, tuck spokes to the inside of the basket following the arrow design. Usually one of the group of 4 can be tucked; however, not always. Trim remaining spokes even with the top of the rim row. A small flat screwdriver or bent tip tool will help with this step. Next, measure around the top outside rim opening of the basket adding 2" for an overlap; cut a piece of 1/2" flat oval reed, shave the end for a neat overlap and soak until flexible. Measure the inside opening, add 2" for overlap, shave, cut, and soak along with medium chair cane or flat oval rim lacer/lasher.

11. Start to the left of the handle and place the flat oval reed with flat side against the basket and oval side facing the outside. Secure with clothespins or clamps, then add inside rim piece, adjust clothespins as needed. Add seagrass rim filler in between the two rim pieces starting at the handle. Add plastic cable ties for a tight fit, remove during lashing.

12. Tuck the end of cane lacer or waxed linen under the inside rim at the handle. Lace/lash around the basket rim between every 2 spokes. Continue until reaching the starting point, tuck end, and trim.

13. **FINISHING TOUCHES:** Clip any fuzzy fibers on your finished basket for a neat appearance. Be sure to personalize the base of the completed basket by signing your name and/or initials, and date or number the basket for future reference.

14. **HANDLE WRAP OPTION:** See instructions for the Chevron "V" Arrow Wrap to complement the twill arrow design in the basket.

15. **STAIN OPTIONS:** Once the finished basket is dry, choose to stain with natural walnut hull dye or another dye or oil of your choice.

CHEVRON "V" ARROW HANDLE WRAP
Materials
Handle
1/4" flat reed – handle wrapper
Medium cane – arrow
2 pieces 3/16" or 1/4" dyed reed – "handle anchors"

Procedure

1. Wet all pieces before wrapping the handle. Measure and mark the center of the top arch of the handle for X later.

2. Tuck end of long piece of 1/4" flat reed under inside of rim at the handle. At the same time, place two pieces of 3/16" or 1/4" dyed accent reed anchors on the outside of the handle and tuck under the outside rim.

3. Wrap around the handle and over the dyed reed for 2 or more rows.

4. Begin arrow handle wrap design with a long piece of medium cane. Slide cane under the two pieces of dyed reed "anchors" (between the handle) with right side of cane touching handle, wrong side facing out. Pull cane until halfway.

5. Now with the cane secured, wrap above the cane with flat reed handle wrapper over dyed reed anchors for 2 rows. Then take 2 ends of cane and weave on a diagonal over these 2 rows of wrapper, and to the center of the handle to meet the arrow. Ends are taken under 1/4" dyed anchor pieces and bent to the outside of the handle with wrong sides of cane facing up. Let these cane ends hang loosely as you continue to wrap 2 rows above with flat reed wrapper for the next arrow.

OPTION: You may choose to continue the arrow wrap in the same direction all the way across the handle, or, continue the arrow wrap design until you reach the center mark. At this point, the arrow can be reversed by securing the cane pieces under one row of handle wrapper when they meet in the center. Continue the handle wrapper for 2 rows (wraps), the cane pieces will now move on a diagonal from the center to the outside of the handle and bend into the center (wrong side facing up), under the 1/4" dyed reed to secure. This makes a long "X" at the center of the handle and reverses the design. Continue the cane pieces coming from the outside edges to the center and hang loosely while wrapping 2 times with flat handle wrapper.

6. Continue wrapping the handle until 1" remains. To end the wrapper, bring cane pieces and tuck under the two 1/4" dyed handle pieces and wrap for 2 or more times to complete the handle wrap. Tuck handle wrapper inside the basket rim.

Projects

Gourds

2.5: Triple Pine Needle

by Charlotte Durrence

This project is for those who have some experience weaving with pine needles and working with gourds. Choose a martin gourd that sits straight and is rather tall. Clean the gourd by soaking it in water for fifteen minutes and scrubbing the mold off with a pot scrubber.

Supplies Needed

Materials

Martin gourd

Pine needles – dyed or natural

Artificial sinew or waxed linen thread

Tapestry needle

Triple Pine Needle by Charlotte Durrence.
Photography by Derral Durrence.

Procedure

1. Mark the gourd with a pencil, around the top and make in a "u" shape in front.

2. Using a mini jigsaw, cut, following the line.

3. Clean out the inside of the gourd and sand it if necessary.

4. At this point you may paint or otherwise finish the inside of the gourd.

5. If you choose to put a finish on the outside of the gourd, you will do this before you begin coiling.

6. Drill holes around the top of the gourd 1/4 of an inch from the top of the rim and about 3/8 of an inch apart.

7. Thread a tapestry needle with artificial sinew. Cut the sinew as long as you can comfortable work with it. You will sew with a single thread, so do not put a knot in the thread.

8. Always work from the outside to the inside with the needle.

9. Pick up 2 pine needles each time you go through a hole in the bowl.

10. Tie the first 2 caps onto the bowl and make a knot, so that they will not come loose. I usually start at the back of the bowl.

11. The cap ends should be even with the hole to the right of the hole you are using.

12. Put the needle into the hole and pull it tight, making sure you catch the cap ends in the loop before you pull it tight. **It is very important that you keep the thread tight at all times.**

13. If you are left-handed, you may want to reverse these directions.

14. Continue around the gourd adding 2 pine needles at each hole until you reach the beginning. At that point you will need to continue sewing for about 6 holes without adding pine needles.

15. Put the 1/2 inch gage onto the remaining ends of the pine needles.

16. This is the point where you will begin to add pine needles from which you have removed the caps. Add them into the middle of the gage so that the ends never show.

17. Continue sewing by using the last stitch as a guide to know where to put your needle through the previous row.

18. When you get to the place where you want the rim to flow freely, just wrap the thread around the coil as evenly as you can.

19. Begin attaching it to the other side of the "u" shape so that it is even with the opposite side.

20. Continue around the rim in the same manner and make another free flowing area in the "u" shape.

21. At this point you can probably stop adding pine needles to the gage.

22. Continue sewing until all of the ends are sewn down. Knot your thread.

2.6: Coiled Cherokee Basket

by Shirley Thomason

You will need pine needle coiling experience for this intermediate to advanced basket. You will need to be experienced cleaning a gourd, or purchase one already cleaned and cut.

Cherokee Basket by Shirley Thomason. Photography by Jennifer Coker.

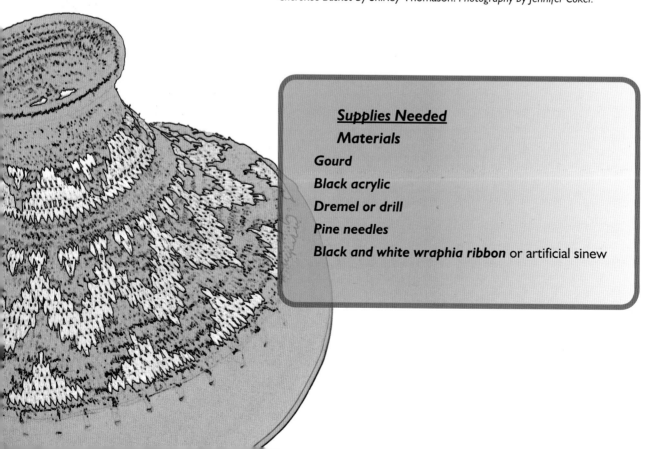

Supplies Needed

Materials

Gourd

Black acrylic

Dremel or drill

Pine needles

Black and white wraphia ribbon or artificial sinew

Procedure

Step 1: Starting with a gourd that has been cleaned, inside and out, paint the inside and outside with black acrylic. After it is dry, use a Dremel tool and a small bit to make holes about 1/4" to 1/8" apart. Once the holes are drilled, use black wraphia ribbon and about five complete pine needle pieces. Threading a large tapestry needle, wrap the black wraphia ribbon around the five pine needle pieces, going through the needles and back out. This secures the ribbon to the needles. Wrap the needles for about 1/8", then hold them up against the gourd and go through the first hole from the back. Go through the hole one more time and then through the section that was just wrapped. This secures the wrap. Continue to wrap around the sections, but not attaching them until coming to the next hole. Go through the hole, come out and go through again and attach. Do this all the way around the first row until coming back to where you started. The first row is very important and slow, but it is the basis for your whole basket. You will also need to remember to add pine needles about every six wraps, so your bundle of pine needles remains the same length and width. If you don't remember this, you will work yourself out of needles and it will not look good. So be diligent about adding them. You just remove the head of the pine needle with scissors, and stick the new ones inside the middle of the bundle. Once you get this done, you can then start to plan your design.

Step 2: The second row is started using all white wraphia ribbon. You will go from back to front, going around the previous row, stitching each wrap onto the previous coil. Do this until you come around to the end of the second row. As you work your rows you will want to hold each row slightly in as you stitch so it is gradually working itself inwards.

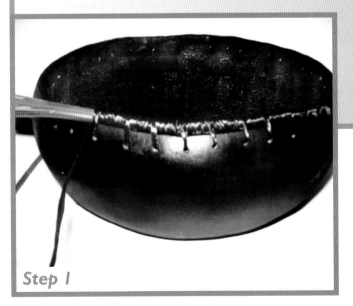

Step 1

Step 2

Photos *courtesy of Shirley Thomason.*

Step 3: This is the most important row, the second row or whatever row you are going to start a design. Since black and white ribbon is used, a black marker will mark where the geometric design starts. Think of the circle you have in front of you like a pie. Do you want 4 designs, 6 design, 8 designs, 10 designs and so on. You will use your marker and make a small mark onto the white raffia, much like you would be slicing a pie. Do 4 first, then if you want 8, do them, and so on.

Step 3

Step 4: Now threading black wraphia ribbon, make 4 to 5 wraps for each part of the design. You will have to drop the black and add the white, which will be threaded on another needle. Drop one thread by going through the coil and back and then cutting in the back of the gourd. Then attach the new thread right next to the other, leaving a tail hanging in the back of the gourd. You can trim these after the basket is finished. Once you have your first row, the next row will become slightly longer. If you started with 4, make it 8, two on either side of the 4 and so on. You will continue until the white is the smallest thread left. That will be your last row with this pattern.

Step 4

Step 5: On the next row, you will work it to look like the last row, but in the middle of the row, you will put 1 or 2 wraps of the white and then switch to the black and make it look like the last row. Looking at the picture you can see it's like having a white row growing within the black row. This is actually a very complicated design, and you will have to keep your mind on it as you go.

Step 5

Step 6: The next row, you will make the white row grow like you did the black row when you first started, and still using the black until it becomes the smallest.

Step 7: You will revert back to the black design again. You will note that the basket is coming in and the design is getting smaller.

Step 8: You will continue to do your design. End this second design with 2-3 rows of just black. Bring the basket in and up. Only one more small design can be made. Once it is in as far as you want, go up with the design to create a vase look, using only the black until it is the size you want.

Step 9: When you have gone around and want to come to your last row, you must stop adding pine needles inside the wraps, so that you can narrow it down. Some people when they are coiling just stop when they come to the last wrap, but this does not look good. When you are within the last 4-5 stitches, using scissors, cut the pine needles to a point so that as you wrap, it works into the basket so you do not notice the ending as much.

Step 6

Step 7

Step 8

2.7: Devil's Claw Gourd

by Karen Hafer

This is a wonderful fun gourd project for all levels.

Devil's Claw Gourd by Karen Hafer. *Courtesy of Karen Hafer.*

Supplies Needed

Materials

Gourd – cut and cleaned, 7" diameter and 11" high

Artificial sinew, natural

Artificial sinew or waxed linen thread, black

Date palm fruit stalks

Yarn

Jute

Unraveled seagrass

Split palm leaves (dried)

Dried gourd seeds, uniform in size, painted black

Glass beads

Leather dye

Clear acrylic spray

Devil's claw, dried, painted black (you may grow your own or purchase from suppliers of natural materials). The devil's claw got its name because its fruit will readily cling to animals' hooves or your shoes if you should step on them. The plant is also called the "unicorn plant," since the pod is hornlike before it splits open. Many Native American tribes of the Southwest still use the green or dried pods today for food and in basketry.

Procedure

1. In the sides of the gourd, cut 7 slits of 1" by 4" in measurement. Sand the rough spots.

2. Paint the gourd with leather dye, let dry, and spray with clear acrylic sealer.

3. Using an awl or drill, make holes around the rim 7/8" from the top and 7/8" apart.

4. Weave in and out of the slits on the gourd, using the yarn, jute, unraveled seagrass, split palm leaves, and date palm fruit stalks.

Rim treatment

1. Wrap the rim of the gourd with date palm fruit stalks. Use a needle with artificial sinew and stitch the materials around the gourd with the sinew, going through the holes.

2. Use a needle to pierce a gourd seed for each hole around the rim and attach them with the sinew, adding a glass bead on the outside, then bringing the needle around the bead and back to the inside of the gourd.

3. Attach the painted devil's claw with black artificial sinew or black waxed linen thread.

2.8: Reverse Spirals

This is a beautifully woven gourd that creates spirals and reverse spirals in the weaving. This is called a chevron. The technique is three rod wale or triple twine using dyed reed. The gourd has been wood burned and oil pencil added for color. A small yellow stone has been inlaid for a nice effect. It is an intermediate to advanced weaving project. It helps to know three rod wale (triple twine).

Supplies Needed
Materials:

#3 round reed for spokes (natural, smoked, or a color other than the weavers)

#2 round reed for weavers (two different colors other than the spokes—one will be color #1 and the other will be color #2)

Medium size canteen gourd— around six to eight inches diameter

For design on front, you will need a temperature controlled wood burner, oil pencils, tortillions (paper stubs), spray fixative, and spray sealer

Oval wooden base

Reverse Spirals Chevron.
Photography by Kelly Hazel.

Preparing the gourd

1. Clean the gourd. Use Comet® cleanser and an S.O.S.® pad. Wet the gourd, sprinkle cleanser on it and let it sit for 10 minutes. Clean with pad. Dry.

2. Decide where you want to cut the top of the gourd off. Cut where the top will be level. Mark with a pencil, making sure it is even all the way around. I use a leveler used for marking Nantucket rims.

3. Start by using a drill or knife to make an opening on the pencil line just large enough to insert the saw blade. Cut carefully around the gourd, making sure to stay on the pencil line. Cut the top flat, not at an angle.

4. MAKE SURE YOU ARE WEARING A MASK OR A RESPIRATOR AND IN A VENTILATED AREA! Remove the seeds and clean the inside. Scrape away all loose fibers. You can even sand the inside with a sander or wire brush attachment on a drill and with sandpaper. You can also put water in the gourd and let it sit until the inside loose pieces will come out.

5. On the flat top of the gourd where you cut, make marks with a pencil 1/2" apart all the way around. * The spoke number needs to be divisible by three minus one. Examples are 23, 26, 29, 32, 35, 38, 41, 44, etc.

6. Use an awl and make starting points for all the holes to be drilled. Do this in the center of each mark. Drill each hole carefully. Drill at a slight angle toward the outside of the gourd, and try not to drill out the side of the gourd.

7. Using wood glue, glue spokes in the holes. Let dry completely before weaving. Try not to get glue on top and outside of gourd. Dip the end of the spoke in the glue and wipe off any excess after inserting into hole.

Photography by Kelly Hazel.

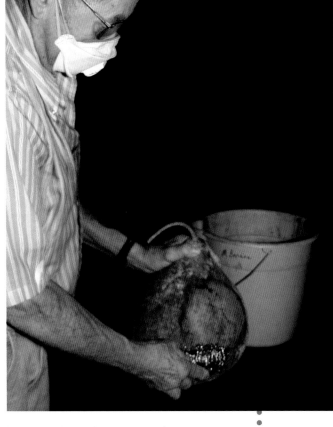

My husband, Jim, cleaning a gourd.

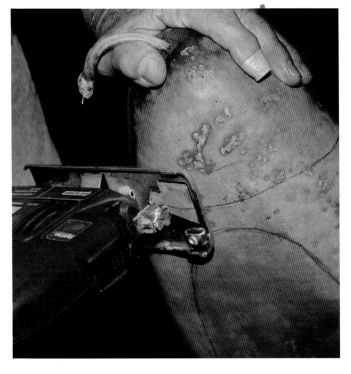

Jim sawing the gourd.

Jim cleaning the inside of the gourd.

Gluing the spokes in the hole.

Drilling the holes in the top of the gourd
for the spokes.

*__Alternate:__ If you have a gourd that is not thick
enough to put the spokes on the top, you
can still weave on it. The spokes will just be
inserted differently. Make your spokes twice
the length that you would for a spoke going
on top of the gourd. Drill your holes around
the side of the gourd, 1/4" down from the
top and 1/2" apart. You will need to wet your
spokes as they will be bent. Fold your spoke
in half and gently use needle nose pliers to
break the fibers. From the inside of the gourd
place one end of the spoke through one hole
and the other end through the very next hole.
Pull both ends gently through the holes to the
outside with the bend in the center. Flatten
the bend against the inside of the gourd. Do
this with each spoke. If you have an uneven
number of holes, cut a spoke in half and insert
one end inside the gourd behind a loop made
by the bent part of the last spoke. Then pull
the other end through the last hole to the
outside of the gourd.

Weaving Triple Twine

1. Mark three consecutive spokes with ribbon or twist ties or you can bend down the three spokes at the top about 1/4". In the triple twine technique you will need to know where the beginning spoke is located. Since you do have to add to the weavers when they run out, you will have a hard time finding the beginning spoke just by looking inside the basket. Place the three weavers of color #1 behind each marked spoke.

2. Take the weaver that is behind the first marked spoke to the left. It goes in front of the next two spokes, behind the next third spoke, and out again. Now pick up the second weaver, which is now the first weaver to the left. Repeat the same sequence you did with the first weaver: in front of two spokes, in front of the next two weavers, behind the third spoke, and out. This sequence will continue all the way around the gourd basket. Remember to always start with the first weaver to the left and move to the right each time.

Step one in weaving the triple twine.

Take the weaver that is behind the first marked spoke to the left. It goes in front of the next two spokes, behind the next third spoke, and out again.

Now pick up the second weaver, which is now the first weaver to the left. Repeat the same sequence you did with the first weaver.

Repeat the same procedure with the last weaver, which is now the first one to the left.

3. Using this triple twine technique, follow this pattern to weave the basket. Weave three rows of triple twine using three #1 color weavers (blue). Remember to keep your weavers and spokes wet by spraying them often. When you get to the beginning spoke of the fourth row, cut one of the #1 color weavers and replace it with a #2 color weaver (yellow). You will leave a two inch tail on the #1 color weaver and place it behind the spokes. Add the new #2 color weaver in the same place. Continue to triple twine weave for three rows with two #1 color weavers and one #2 color weaver. At the end of the third row, cut the next #1 color weaver and add another #2 color weaver (yellow). Triple twine for three rows with one #1 color weaver and two #2 color weavers. When you finish the three rows and get back to the beginning marked spoke, cut the three spokes and tuck them to the inside of the gourd behind the first three marked spokes. Turn the weavers around and you will be weaving in the reverse direction. Place the three weavers behind the same three spokes and triple twine for 3 rows with 1 of #1 color (blue) and 2 of #2 color (yellow). Then cut one #2 color and add a #1 color (blue) and triple twine for 3 rows. When you finish those rows, cut the last #2 color and weave with three #1 colors (blue) for four or five rows. You are weaving with all three #1 weavers now (blue). When you finish weaving these rows, cut all three spokes and tuck to the inside. Now it is time to do the rim.

This is what a row of triple twine looks like.

Step 1 of the rim.

Step 2 of the rim.

Step 3 of the rim.

The Rim

Soak your spokes well. Running them under warm water or placing upside down in a bucket of water for about five minutes should help. If you have been spraying your spokes throughout the entire weaving process, the spokes should be wet enough. You do not need to wet the weavers or inside the gourd, just the base of the spokes where you will be bending them. You can use needle nose pliers and pinch them close to the weaving. This will help, because you just do not want to break the spokes.

1: Take any three spokes. You will be moving to the right. Place the spoke to the left behind the two to the right and down to the front of the basket.

2: Pick up a new spoke to have three and repeat this sequence. Continue this weaving all the way around the gourd.

3: When you have only two spokes left, loosen the first loop to the right and put the left spoke through it.

4: Then loosen the second loop to the right and put the last spoke through it. Tighten both loops to finish the first step.

5: The next step is to go over two spokes that are sticking out the front and then go inside the basket through the hole made by the first row. This hole is right beside the third spoke to the right. Continue all the way around until you have two spokes left. Pull the first two spokes out a little and place the last two spokes through those holes. Tighten the loops just like in the first step. Cut the ends of the spokes that are inside the basket. Stitch philodendron sheaths over the rim with waxed linen thread. You can add pods or beads as decoration.

Also step 3 of the rim.

Step 4 of the rim.

This is what it looks like when you finish steps 1-4.

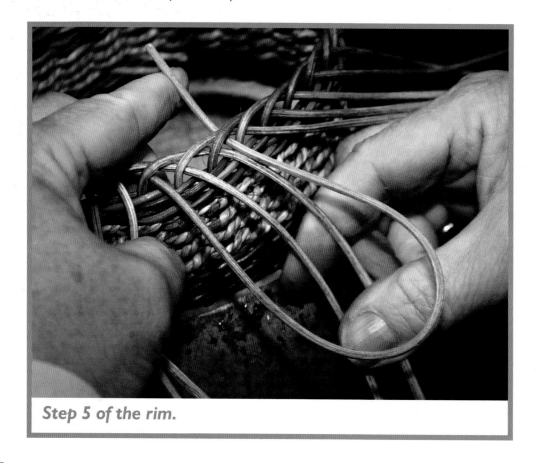

Step 5 of the rim.

2.9: Coiled Iris Leaves on Gourd

by Gloria Christian

In mid- and late summer through early fall, I pull the bottom leaves of the iris plant off when they die. This is a beginner to intermediate pattern.

Coiled Iris Leaves on Gourd by Gloria Christian. *Courtesy of Gloria Christian.*

> ### Supplies Needed
> **Materials:**
> *Iris leaves*
>
> *Gourd*
>
> *Glycerin*
>
> *Sinew or wax linen*
>
> *Needle*

Preparation of Gourd

Mark a line 1/4 to 1/3 of the way down and draw a wavy/scalloped line with one side 1 to 2 inches higher. Cut the gourd, clean, and sand. Drill holes 1/4" down and 1/2" apart. You can use a brown tone shoe polish to match the colors within the leaves. Buff to a shine, and/or spray or brush on light coat of sealer.

Preparation of Leaves

Soak in warm water for about 5 minutes to soften and rinse to remove dirt and pollen. Soak again in warm water and a tablespoon of glycerin for another 5 minutes to make sure all leaves are moistened, stirring occasionally. Pat dry leaves so they are not dripping wet.

Coiling the Basket

Use 2 to 3 yards of sinew, wax linen or other materials for stitching (more may be needed to finish), in black or brown. Insert needles and sinew from the inside to outside and tie a knot. Go through the next hole from the inside to outside. Gather around 3 to 4 leaves together, position the leaves just above the hole and stitch around the leaves going from inside to outside and make the stitch tight. This tight stitch gathers the leaves together to create multiple colors of browns. Continue stitching around and adding leaves to keep the same thickness. To layer the leaves, when you have reached your beginning spot, continue stitching, not through the gourd holes as before, but through 1/4 of the leaves and the bottom stitch. When you have several layers, discontinue adding leaves, but continue stitching until you run out of leaves and knot the thread. You may add natural materials of your choice for embellishments. Spray a light coat of sealer to add shine and sheen to the leaves.

I have many wonderful basket makers and gourd artists who contributed to this book. Their work is incredible and shows the uses of many varied and different materials. I am totally amazed at how many exciting materials weavers and coilers use in their creations. Here is a gallery of some of mine and their work.

Miniature Gretchen Rim Gourds using waxed linen thread by Charlotte Durrence.
Photography by Derral Durrence.

Seagrass Lidded Gourd by Dianne Schuler.
Photography by Beth Liner.

Sea Turtle by Gail Bishop. Gail used seagrass for the rim.
Courtesy of Gail Bishop.

Akosia, 11" x 8" x 8". Akosia is the name of all Ghanaian woman born on Sunday. She is woven with cotton paper, wire, Ghanaian batik fabric, and recycled glass beads. *Courtesy of Jackie Abrams.*

Celebration by Peggy Wiedemann.
Photography by Jan Seeger.

Gourd With Tapestry by Marla Helton.
Photography by Stuart A. Fabe.

Gourd With Yucca by Marla Helton.
Photography by Stuart A. Fabe.

KamiAmi Woman by Jackie Abrams. 8" height. This piece was
created in Ghana, using recycled plastic bags and palm leaves, as
Jackie worked with the KamiAmi Women.
Courtesy of Jackie Abrams.

*Random Weave With Bark
Covered Wire* by Marla Helton.
Photography by Stuart A. Fabe.

Slinky by *Peggy* Wiedemann.
Photography by Jan Seeger.

Silver Twill by Jackie Abrams. 4" x 6" x 6". Traditional
cathead basket, woven of painted cotton paper.
Courtesy of Jackie Abrams.

Woven Basket on Base by Marla Helton.
Photography by Stuart A. Fabe.

Turtle Gourd Basket by Shirley Thomason.
Photography by Jennifer Coker.

Women of Many Cultures by Jackie
Abrams. 10" x 6" x 6" (on left), 8.5"
x 5" x 5". Woven of painted cotton
paper, wire, and fabrics from many
cultures: Bali, Japan, India, and Ghana.
Courtesy of Jackie Abrams.

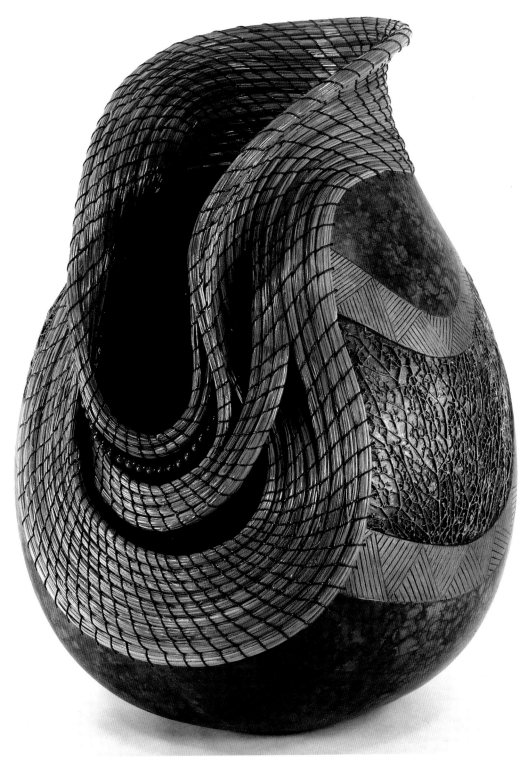

Cactus by Judy Richie. The gourd has pine needle coiling
on top and on the gourd itself, cactus fiber has been glued.
Courtesy of Judy Richie.

Gourd Coiled Basket by Shirley Thomason.
Photography by Jennifer Coker.

Wired Arch by Don Weeke. 12 1/2" x 10 1/2" x 4". Gourd, magnet wire, paint. Knotless netting.
Photography by Rodney Nakamoto.

Diamond Basket by Don Weeke. 27" x 26" x 26".
Gourd, rattan, oak, paint. Weaving and pyrography.
Photography by Rodney Nakamoto.

One Up, Two Down by Don Weeke. 30 1/2" x 13"
x 13". Gourds, paint, reed, king palm seed frond.
Weaving technique.
Photography by Rodney Nakamoto.

Ruth's Sunflower by Don Weeke. 13 1/2" x 13" x 13".
Gourd, paint, date palm seed frond. Techniques:
couching, coiling, carving, pyrography.

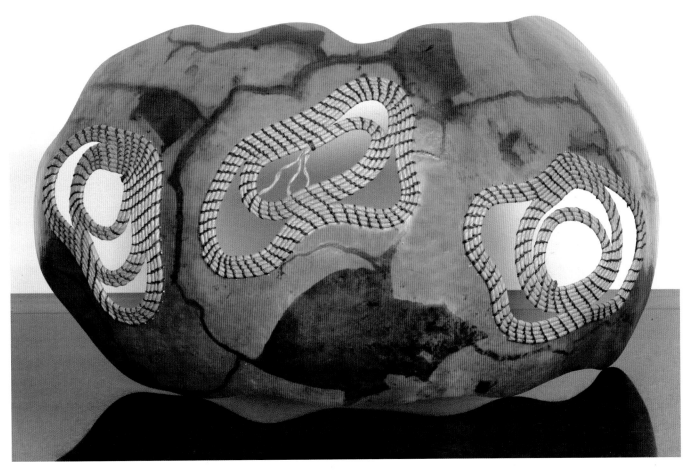

Breastplate by Stuart A. Fabe. Gourd and Danish cord. Coiling technique.
Courtesy of Stuart A. Fabe.

Woven gourd by Terri Schmit. Seagrass, wire, and aventurine with open
and closed coiling. *Courtesy of Terri Schmit.*

Heritage Bowl by Stuart A. Fabe. Gourd and Danish cord. Coiling technique.
Courtesy of Stuart A. Fabe.

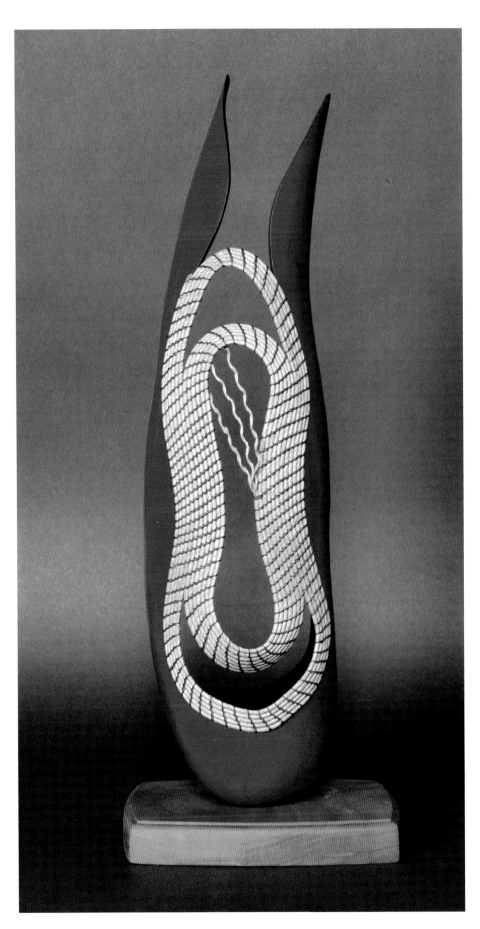

Amber Wave by
Stuart A. Fabe.
Gourd and Danish
cord. Coiling
technique. *Courtesy
of Stuart A. Fabe.*

Nubia by Stuart A. Fabe. Gourd and Danish cord. Coiling technique.
Courtesy of Stuart A. Fabe.

Tillamook by Stuart A. Fabe. Gourd and Danish cord. Coiling technique.
Courtesy of Stuart A. Fabe.

Woven gourd by Terri Schmit. Walnut petioles and seagrass coiling.
Courtesy of Terri Schmit.

Spiral Kimono by Don Weeke. 14" x 20" x 11". Gourds, paint, date palm seed frond. Techniques are couching, coiling, and pyrography. *Photography by Tom Henderson.*

Sweetgrass coiled on gourds by Angie Wagner.
Courtesy of Angie Wagner.

Pine needles coiled on gourds by Angie Wagner.
Courtesy of Angie Wagner.

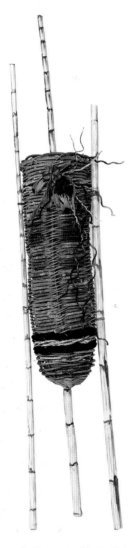

Currents in Nature by Marla Helton. Bamboo
legs, vine rattan, coconut fiber, and seagrass.
Photography by Stuart A. Fabe.

Chase Coil Weave by Marla Helton.
Variegated seagrass and Danish cord.
Photography by Stuart A. Fabe.

Sculptural Harmony by Marla Helton. Danish cord and twig.
Photography by Stuart A. Fabe.

Watercolor paper baskets made by Sandra Roback.
Photography by Kelly Hazel.

Driftwood Basket by Maxine Riley. Made with
jute, reed, grapevine, and philodendron sheath.
Photography by Kelly Hazel.

Lotus Teapot by Donna Sakamoto Crispin. Made of red cedar bark, NW sedge, sweetgrass, and curly filbert branch. *Courtesy of Donna Sakamoto Crispin.*

Nucleus by Polly Jacobs Giacchina is made of date palm and bamboo, 18" x 15" x 14".
Photography by Rodney Nakamoto.

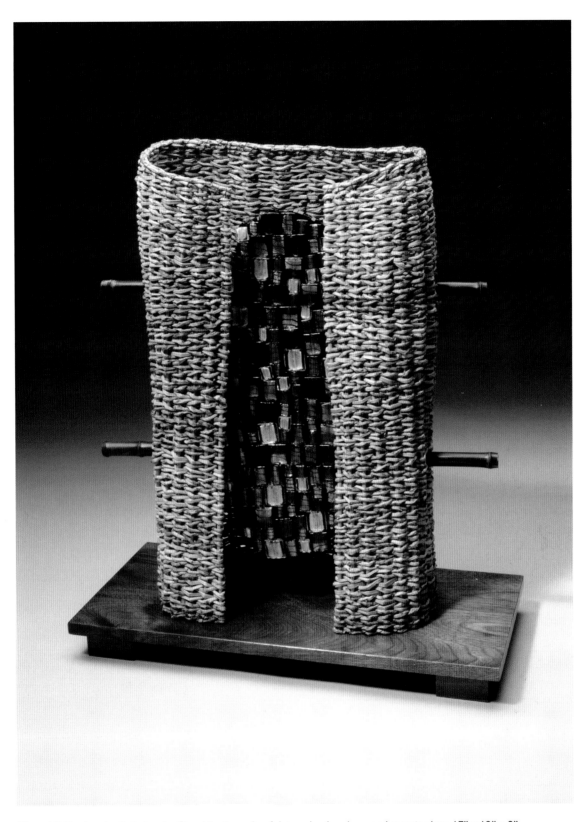

Pierced Reflections by Polly Jacobs Giacchina is made of date palm, bamboo, and mosaic glass, 17" x 12" x 8".
Photography by Rodney Nakamoto.

Tubular Wire With Bead Inserts by Marla Helton.
Photography by Stuart A. Fabe.

Frogs by author. Top woven with dyed paper cording and waxed linen thread. *Photography by Kelly Hazel.*

Gourd woven with wire by Laraine Short. Glass used for embellishments. *Photography by Kelly Hazel.*

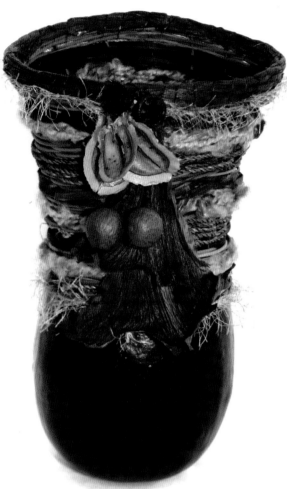

Woven gourd by Penny Reynolds. Yarns, seagrass, philodendron sheath, and pods were used to weave the gourd. *Photography by Kelly Hazel.*

Wall hanging by Cass Schorsch. The loom is warped with 20 gauge copper, then the body of the piece is woven with cedar and copper, along with some other barks such as spruce, red pine, and white pine. Dyed seagrass and roving adds color. *Courtesy of Cass Schorsch.*

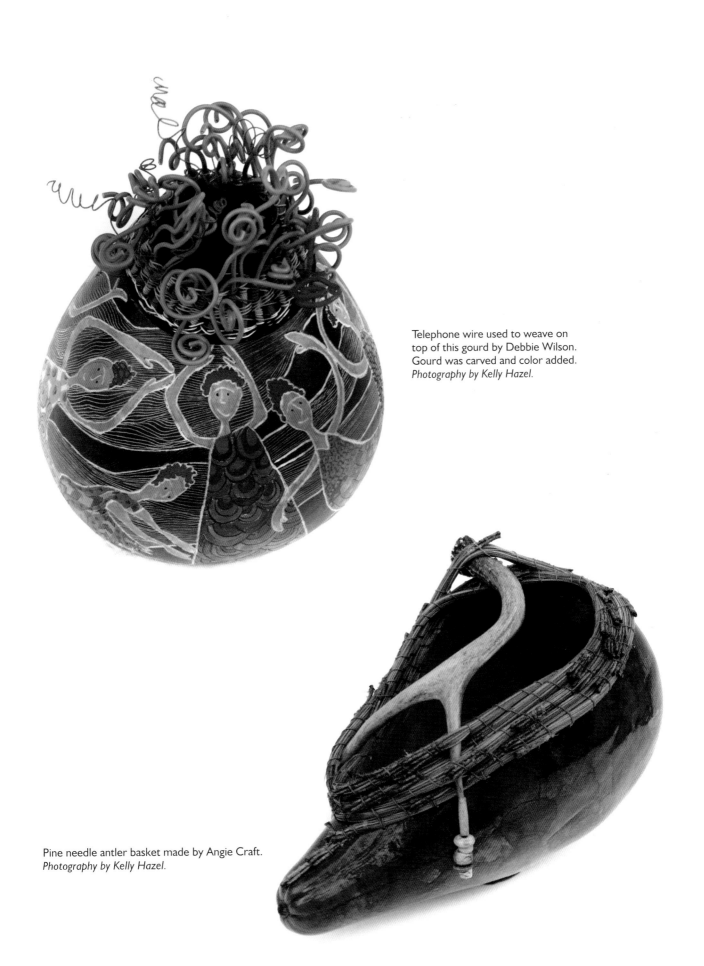

Telephone wire used to weave on top of this gourd by Debbie Wilson. Gourd was carved and color added. *Photography by Kelly Hazel.*

Pine needle antler basket made by Angie Craft. *Photography by Kelly Hazel.*

Undulated Spiral by the author. Materials: Dyed seagrass, dyed reed, philodendron sheath, waxed linen thread, jacaranda pod, and glass beads. *Photography by Kelly Hazel.*

Silver wire, black wire, and beads used for the weaving on this gourd by Debbie Wilson. Gourd was painted and carved. *Photography by Kelly Hazel.*

Earth Spirit Basket by Jaynie Barnes. Natural and synthetic fibers: Seagrass, dyed red hemp and yarn with dyed pod. *Courtesy of Jaynie Barnes.*

Small pine needle basket with glycerin needles
on a tree wood base by Nancy Basket.
Photography by Kelly Hazel.

Forest by the author. Materials:
Reed, seagrass, yarns, cedar bark,
philodendron sheath, waxed linen
thread, jacaranda pod, beads.
Photography by Kelly Hazel.

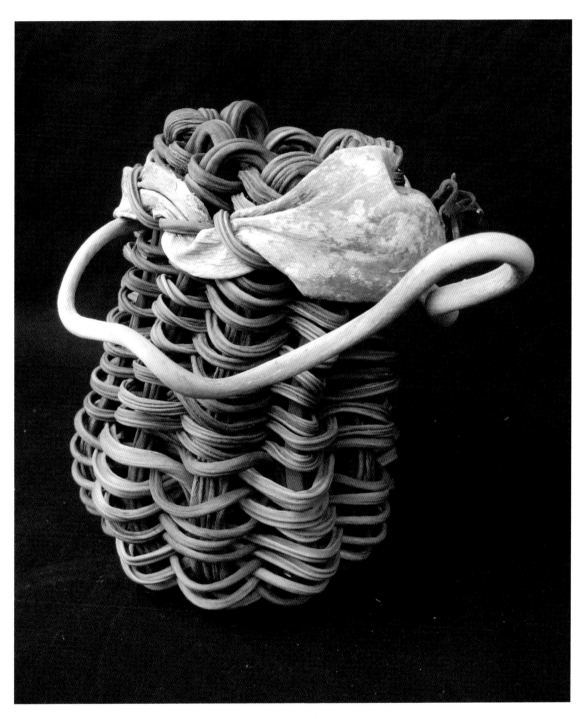

Bull Whip Kelp Basket by Gerri (Gairaud) Swanson.
Courtesy of Gerri (Gairaud) Swanson

Medicine Basket by Jaynie Barnes. 11" x 8". Gourd with dreamcatcher, natural fibers, antler, leather pouch, beads, and bone feather. Fibers include: dyed hemp (dark brown), seagrass, and dyed jute (lighter brown).
Courtesy of Jaynie Barnes.

Ash purse made by the author. *Photography by Kelly Hazel.*

Mini Knotless Netting Pots by Jaynie Barnes. Knotless netting and coiled waxed linen on top with glass beads. *Courtesy of Jaynie Barnes.*

Ross by Polly Adams Sutton. The basket was
made with cedar bark, cane, and wire.
Courtesy of Polly Adams Sutton.

Cactus Gourd by Judy Richie. The gourd has pine needle coiling
on top and on the gourd itself, cactus fiber has been glued.
Courtesy of Judy Richie.

Clamshell Rattle by Donna Sakamoto Crispin. Made of western red cedar, embroidery floss, and copper wire. *Courtesy of Donna Sakamoto Crispin.*

Canyons and Rain Clouds Tray by Pati English. This basket is made with all round reed. It is a Hopi Wedding plaque. The canyons were depicted in green and gold, while the black and natural symbolize rain clouds. In the Hopi tradition it was woven with several different plant materials from rabbitbrush and other shrubs. *Photography by Kelly Hazel.*

Woven gourd by Bonnie Gibson. Woven with reed and copper wire.
Courtesy of Bonnie Gibson.

Pine needle gourd by Gail Bishop. *Courtesy of Gail Bishop.*

Sampler Basket by the author. Reed and beads were used. Techniques are twining, Japanese weave, inserting beads, and pyrography. *Photography by Kelly Hazel.*

Sampler Seven With Cherokee Wheels by Pati English. *Photography by Kelly Hazel.*

Group of woven gourds by Judie Richie. Left gourd is woven with a relative of the southern sweetgrass, common name is Gulf Muhly. Also stems from the tree, Palo Verde, bark from the mountain cedar or ash juniper, and iris leaves. A slice of Osage orange was added. Gourd in back: Woven with date palm and broom corn. Right Gourd: Juniper ash, date palm, and philodendron sheath. *Courtesy of Judie Richie.*

Opposites Attract by Peggy Wiedemann.
Photography by Jan Seeger.

By the Sea by the author. Materials: Reed, seagrass, yarns, cedar bark, chenille sticks, philodendron sheath, jacaranda pod. Dreamcatcher woven with waxed linen thread. Ash fish were woven and added. *Photography by Kelly Hazel.*

Teapot by Donna Sakamoto Crispin. *Courtesy of Donna Sakamoto Crispin.*

Small Indulgence by Pamela Zimmerman.
Horsehair, sinew, metal.
Photography by Ronald L. Sowers Photography.

Coiled Wire Basket With Beads by
Donna Sakamoto Crispin.
Courtesy of Donna Sakamoto Crispin.

Antler and pine needle basket by Charlotte Durrence.
Photography by Derral Durrence.

Dressed for Success by Pamela Zimmerman.
Horsehair, gourd, artificial sinew, and crystals.
Photography by Ronald L. Sowers Photography.

Three minis by Nancy Basket. Pine needle tray,
oak basket, and a gourd with pine needle rim.
Photography by Kelly Hazel.

Woven gourd by Penny Reynolds.
Photography by Kelly Hazel.

Coiled pine needle gourd by
Laraine Short. *Photography by Kelly
Hazel.*

Antler gourd basket by Angie Craft. *Photography by Kelly Hazel.*

Woven top gourd by Laraine Short. *Photography by Kelly Hazel.*

Biographies of Contributing Artists

Jackie Abrams

www.jackieabrams.com

I have been a maker, mostly of baskets, for over thirty years. I have perfected my skills and consistently challenge myself to create new works. Sitting in my studio, with materials in hand, is always a source of fulfillment, meditation, frustration, and satisfaction. "Women Forms," a series of woven vessels, speak of the cultures and the women I have encountered that have had an impact on my life. The forms reflect connections and relationships, the changing roles of women, shared stories, and ways in which women live and learn.

To create my newest pieces, "Spirit of Women," I use the ancient technique of coiling found almost universally in African societies. This work is evolving. I use the materials at hand and work intuitively, letting the form develop as it grows. Each coil captures the experience of the moment. The form develops a shape, coil by coil, experience by experience. My years of work and travel in Africa, especially in Ghana, have had a profound influence on my work and on my life. I am learning to simplify things, to state what is important. This is what I hope to express in the work I create.

Jaynie Barnes

Earth Spirit Designs
Jmbsunshine20@yahoo.com

Jaynie has been growing and crafting gourds for ten years and teaching for six. Her first exposure to gourds and gourd craft was about 12 years ago when she began collecting gourd rattles from different cultures. As an avid gardener, she soon began growing and crafting her own gourds. Although, initially self taught, she has studied with nationally renowned gourd artists. As a basket maker of many years, she now incorporates her basketry techniques into her gourd art.

She has previously taught at Holyoke Creative Arts Center and Smith College. Her work has been exhibited at the Smith College Campus Center and the Smith College Art Museum. Jaynie's art is featured in two forthcoming art books published in fall, 2010 by Schiffer Publishing, Ltd.: *Antlers in Basketry and Gourd Art* by Betsey Sloan and *Weaving on Gourds* by Marianne Barnes. She currently teaches adult classes and youth workshops at Hill Institute in Florence, Massachusetts.

Jaynie is a member of the Hilltown Artisan Guild, the Shelburne Arts Cooperative, the Center for Native American Awareness, the American Gourd Society, the Pennsylvania Gourd Society, and a twenty year member of the Northampton Community Gardens. Jaynie holds a BA in Education, with twenty years experience facilitating/leading groups and workshops. She is passionate about bringing awareness to gourd culture and gourd art to local communities and the New England area.

Nancy Basket

Kudzu Cabin Designs
www.nancybasket.com

Nancy comes from Yakima, Washington, and takes her name from the work she does and from a paternal Cherokee grandmother, Margaret Basket. She moved to South Carolina in 1989 to gather pine needles for the baskets her friend taught her to make ten years earlier and to to learn Cherokee stories of respect to teach her children. After the stories told her how to talk to the leaves, she found kudzu spoke in a way she understood. This vine eats the South, yet became a dominant source for her artistic expression.

As an artist in education for more than twenty years, Nancy received the South Carolina Jean Laney Harris Folk Heritage award for Cherokee baskets. Her studio and gallery are open to visitors in Walhalla, South Carolina. The kudzu bale barn in her backyard holds her papermaking plant and facilitates classes on basket making, papermaking, and storytelling.

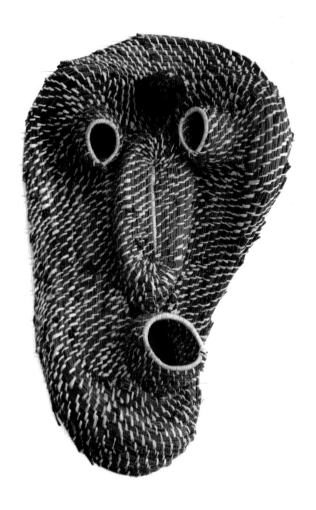

Gail Bishop

GB Dragonfly Designs
GailBishop469@
gourdartenthusiasts.ning.com

I am a native Californian dabbling in art and craft since childhood. I have been working for over twenty-five years in the veterinary field and, because of a injured cat, yes a cat—"Ms. Princess Puss," I met her owner (2007) who was carrying a gourd purse! Having to know all about it, I took her up on an offer and came to a class. There was no turning back! I developed severe rheumatoid arthritis; to help deal with pain, sleepless nights, and to keep functioning, I had taken up jewelry making. Now I incorporate jewelry with gourds and have met so many wonderful people. Gourds and art have become my therapy. I just love working with this great medium and all that can be done with it. Thank you, to my special friend, Gloria Crane.

Angie Craft

Country Craft Gourds & More
www.countrycraftgourds.com

Angie Craft lived most of her life in Hendersonville, North Carolina, until ten years ago when she moved to Pelzer, South Carolina. She has done almost every "arts and crafts" you can think of, and then one day, discovered the gourd. Right after she discovered gourds, she began to take classes to try and decide what her favorite thing to do with them was. Well, today she uses a lot of deer antlers, pine needles, dried botanicals, and other "naturals" in her creations. She also uses a lot of natural embellishments and various rim treatments on her pieces. Most of her gourds are "outdoorsy" and nature-based. She has been in love with creating gourd art for the past seven years.

Angie became a vendor at the Saturday Downtown Market in Greenville in 2006, and welcomed the birth of her business, Country Craft Gourds. Angie teaches at several gourd festivals in the Southeast, as well as several private venues locally. She is also a member of the South Carolina Gourd Society, Palmetto Gourd Patch, founder of The Travelin' Patch, Florida Gourd Society, and the Georgia Basket Association.

Gloria Christian

Gloria lived in many places but settled down in her home state of Alabama. After high school, she worked some as a freelance photographer, publishing several articles and photographs. After living in Phoenix, Arizona, for three years she learned to appreciate the Native American art and culture.

Gloria saw an article in a magazine about wood burning on a gourd around fourteen years ago. She really liked the way it looked, natural but elegant, thus her gourd art days began. As a self taught artisan, she progressed in carving and other mediums, including wood burning, weaving, inlay, and painting. She enjoys creating colorful one-of-a-kind art. To achieve the look and style she likes, she continues to add new techniques. Her many ribbons were won throughout the fourteen years as a gourd artist. It is a passion that she will continue to learn, teach, and hopefully inspire others to appreciate.

Donna Sakamoto Crispin

Each item I make is unique. I collect wild materials such as twigs, seaweed, leaves, and more, weaving with the Japanese belief that plants have spirits that are passed on through the finished craft, as is the spirit of the basket weaver. I've been weaving for twenty-three years, and teaching workshops for twenty-two years. I've taught people of all ages, from first grade through senior citizens. I offer a variety of basketry classes, including my own personal designs, in addition to papermaking, silk papermaking, and basic bookbinding. I graduated from the University of Illinois at Champaign-Urbana in 1976, and also Utah State University, Logan, 1985. My second degree is in Elementary Education, and since then, I have been working part-time as an Educational Assistant, and as a basket maker.

Charlotte Durrence

www.webgourds.com/southern
(Charlotte is the founder and sponsor of the Gourd Retreat-Southern Style)

I painted my first gourd in 1993 and have been consumed by the desire to do many more. I still have that first gourd. It reminds me of all that I have learned over the years. I am a charter member of the Georgia Gourd Society and have held many offices in the organization. I served as first Vice-President of the American Gourd Society for one term.

Teaching gourd art classes has taken me all over the country and I have met so many wonderful people with the same interest. My husband, Derral, has been a great supporter in all things that I do. I love doing pine needle weaving and natural gourds.

Pati English

Baskets My Specialty
www.BasketsMySpecialty.com

An avid collector of Native American baskets and baskets from around the world, Pati enjoys sharing her love of baskets as a Resident Artist with the South Carolina Arts Commission. Juried baskets of her original designs are included in museums, traveling exhibitions, art shows, and discovery centers in the Southeast. She has earned ribbons at the North Carolina Basket Association Exhibits, fine craft, and purchase awards at juried art shows around the Southeast. Her baskets were featured in Basket Bits Magazine, South Carolina Farmer Magazine, and at The Wren House, in Southern Living Magazine. She appeared on SC-ETV, "On the Road" and RFD-TV "Making It Grow," currently being aired nationwide in "The Best of Making It Grow." Membership in the Southern Arts Federation provides photographs of her work at SouthernArtistry.org. Pati is a member of numerous basket organizations, and stays active with her local basket guild volunteering as President, Convention Coordinator and several board positions. Pati has given lectures as part of the Heritage Lecture Series and programs such as "Baskets Around the World" and served as Guest Curator for the "Traditional and Contemporary Basketry Exhibition," highlighted in the National Basketry Organization Magazine. A former library media specialist, current basket maker and instructor, Pati has enjoyed twenty-four years designing and writing original patterns, inspired by her country landscape. Her patterns are in print and available from several basket suppliers, as well as her website. She continues teaching students of all ages at museums, state conventions, schools, and guilds in South Carolina, North Carolina, Florida, Georgia, Kentucky, Pennsylvania, Tennessee, and Virginia, at the John C. Campbell Folk School and anywhere baskets take her with the hope to keep the art of basketry alive and ensure its place in the twenty-first century.

Stuart Fabe

Stuart Fabe Fine Art
www.stuartfabe.com/index.shtml

Stuart Fabe is a native Ohioan who hails from a family with a rich heritage in the arts. While the majority of his professional career had been devoted to raising charitable funds for several of Cincinnati's most prominent medical centers and cultural institutions, Stuart has been passionate about fine art for over thirty years. He has traveled throughout North America, Europe, the Middle East, and Africa creating highly expressive black & white images, which have generated broad popular appeal. Many of his images render a dreamlike quality created by utilizing the ethereal infrared technique.

Upon retiring from his corporate career, Stuart left Cincinnati for full-time residence on the Indiana farm where his creative sensibilities nurtured a fresh artistic medium. He has mastered the art of dyeing and weaving on hard-shell gourds, which he grows on the quiet Indiana farm that he shares with his partner, Marla, along with two dogs, two cats, and an assortment of other wildlife critters. The fascination with gourds provides an artistic balance between his passion for two-D black & white photographs and the world of "natural sculpture."

Polly Jacobs Giacchina

Polly Jacobs Fiber Sculpture
www.pollyjgfiberart.com

Sculptural forms and structures express my view of art. Weaving with natural materials allows me to respond to my surroundings and develop design ideas. Through this connection I emphasize works that are inspired by the textures, colors, and unique components of nature.

I sculpt using the weaving technique, twining. Pliable natural and industrial materials are used to explore each project. Even the collecting of materials, mainly date palm, is part of the creative process. At times, multiple units are produced and then put together to form relationships. Stronger rigid materials are bent and reformed to seek new possibilities. Reinterpreting and transforming materials creates a more meaningful complex form, to transcend and connect to nature.

Polly Jacobs Giacchina was inspired by Joan Austin at San Diego State University and by artist Misti Washington of Solana Beach, California. Each gave a view of art and fiber that brought on a desire for exploration of natural materials through basketry sculpture. An understanding of nature and sculptural forms has developed over time. Polly has gone on to exhibit nationally and internationally from 1982 to the present, showing her twined sculptures. She has received awards and published recognition and also teaches fiber techniques.

Bonnie Gibson

Arizona Gourd
www.ArizonaGourds.com
bonnie@arizonagourds.com

Bonnie Gibson is an accomplished artist in many forms of three-dimensional arts and fine crafts. Completely self-taught, she has gained recognition for her work in gourds, wood carving, scrimshaw, and scale miniatures, as well as trying her hand at many other art forms. She has earned many awards in different media, including multiple "Best of Show" awards.

"I am a self taught artisan. I prefer this term over "artist," because to me it denotes a person who works with items that can be functional as well as aesthetically pleasing. Even as a child, working with my hands and creating things captivated me. I took art classes in high school, but I always felt more comfortable with three-dimensional creations instead of traditional paintings and drawings. Working with gourds allows me to utilize the technical skills that I've developed over the years while working with other media. Native cultures, wildlife, and nature are my favorite subjects."

Bonnie utilizes many tools and techniques to reach a finished design. Carving, pyrography, painting and inlays of stone make for striking accents to the overall design. Certain design elements such as carved sand ripples, filigree, and basketry effects have become her signature patterns.

Bonnie is a highly sought after and well respected instructor. She has a BS and MS in education, and has taught gourd carving and crafting classes for many years. Bonnie travels extensively, teaching workshops from coast to coast. Her website, ArizonaGourds. com, is a major source of gourd crafting supplies and tools, as well as a wealth of gourd crafting tutorials and information. Bonnie is also the founder of Gourd Art Enthusiasts, an online group for those interested in gourds and gourd art. You can find the web site at http://gourdartenthusiasts.ning.com.

Nancy Gildersleeve

Nancy Gildersleeve has been making baskets for many years, most recently using gathered natural materials: vines, leaves, and tree barks. She teaches pine needle basketry at state parks in north Florida and at the John C. Campbell Folk School and at gourd gatherings in the Southeast. Her work can be seen at the Artisans Guild of Gainesville.

Karen Hafer

Karen has always had an interest in art, crafts, and designing with natural materials, having grown and arranged dried flowers for years. Upon retiring from teaching in elementary school, she studied floral design and now works part-time as a floral designer. Several years ago she became enthralled with gourd art. Since then she has been exploring the variety of techniques possible with the gourd. She especially enjoys weaving on gourds, and the use of many natural materials.

Karen is a member of the American Gourd Society, Pennsylvania Gourd Society, and a local gourd club. She has won numerous blue ribbons for her gourds at county and state fairs.

Marla Helton

Serendipity Gourd Art
http://serendipitygourdart.com

Marla Helton became interested in mixed media in the late 1980s after taking a basket class. She began by combining weaving techniques with pottery pieces and soon moved on to weaving on gourds. She finds her inspiration in the shape and color of the gourd as well as interesting materials that she discovers in many of her travels. Marla does art shows throughout the Midwest and teaches classes at retreats and conventions all over the country. She enjoys encouraging her students to follow their own creative instincts. For more of Marla's work, visit her web site.

Ron Layton

http://ronsprimitiveskills.blogspot.com

I have been involved in primitive skills and wilderness living skills for most of my life. I enjoy hiking, nature, and photography. I am retired and living in the central valley of California. I am a former member of the US Army Special Forces and was trained in wilderness survival skills.

Penny Reynolds

http://gourdartenthusiasts.ning.com/profile/PennyReynolds

Penny Reynolds has enjoyed working with gourds before she knew the gourd "world" and its societies existed. It began in 1998 when she visited Cherokee and one of the stores had a bin filled with gourds. She took one home and created her first piece of gourd art! A self taught artist, Penny felt that after years of working with various mediums, she was very connected to the gourds and in turn her Cherokee ancestors. Penny likes to keep her pieces as natural as possible, with a strong emphasis on Native American art. Her eclectic collection includes chip carving, weaving, wood burning, and natural additions such as pine needles and plant sheaths.

Penny's designs come from the gourd itself, as she says it talks to her. If a completed gourd gives Penny a positive and overwhelming feeling, she knows that she has accomplished her intent. She has traveled with Turtle Feathers for several years and is a national award winning artist.

She is well known for the tiny dream catchers she weaves into miniature gourds. Her first show was at Cherokee and that is where she sold her first gourd! Her work can be viewed on Bonnie Gibson's Gourd Art Enthusiasts.

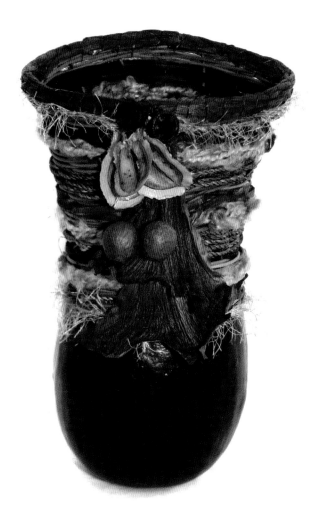

Judy Richie

Redcloud Originals: Fine Gourd Art by Judy Richie
www.redcloudoriginals.com

Judy Richie is a native of Austin, Texas, and has been active in art since an early age. While still in high school she was chosen to attend a summer art camp at the University of Texas with the intent to major in art. A minor detour of marriage, six children, and moving to Colorado and later to Alaska to marry her present husband, Bob, interrupted that goal.

After moving near the small town of Lake City, Colorado, Judy painted and ran her own gallery and later owned and operated a bed and breakfast inn for eight years. She also developed an abiding interest in the art and crafts of the Native Americans, especially those of the Southwest. While living in the small town of Valdez, Alaska, Judy became interested in gourd art and with the help of the Internet in obtaining supplies, books, and articles from varied sources, taught herself the basics of working with gourds. She learned some of her basketry coiling techniques from Aleut and Eskimo women in Alaska. Judy and her husband retired to Kerrville, Texas, in the summer of 2002, where she pursues her art a minimum of thirty hours a week. Discovering the use of gourds for sculptural figures has been a recent delight for Judy's gourd art—most are Native American inspired, several have won major awards. She is becoming known for her uses of patinas with copper, bronze, brass, and silver metal coatings that she uses on the gourds.

Maxine Riley

I began basket weaving as a hobby in 1994. It is most satisfying to craft something by hand. In 1994, I joined the Upper South Carolina Basket Makers Guild, as well as Senior Action.

Both organizations have been wonderful and I learned much. In addition to these groups, I am a member of the South Carolina Gourd Society and the Palmetto Gourd Patch. Weaving and gourds seem to go well together. I love both.

I have had my work juried into Pickens County Museum Exhibition, the Blue Ridge Arts-Seneca, the Arts Alive Show of Senior Action and the South Carolina State Fair. I have won ribbons in all these exhibits.

Sandra Elbrecht Roback

Learning about and making baskets became serious in 1985 and my hands haven't stopped since. I discovered my creative outlet! I have been instructing in basketry for the past few years because I enjoy passing along whatever skills or knowledge I have acquired.

My baskets contain three major design elements: Color, pattern, and form. I enjoy seeing the play of color against color, the dynamics of twill and the challenge of a curved form. I've also been enjoying the challenge of weaving with painted papers. It is important to me that my baskets remain functional even though they may appear decorative. Craftsmanship is also a priority as well as respect for my materials. Hopefully my baskets are pleasing visually as well as tactilely.

Terri Schmit

The Gourd Girl
www.thegourdgirl.com

I have always been a musician. My formal education is in music composition and classical performance. When I met up with my first gourd in 2003 my initial inclination was to use it as a musical instrument, and I did. Within months I was doing the first art I'd ever attempted on one. Gourds have been my only canvas and in these past several years I have gone from simple to complex drawings, done weaving and coiling, carving, burning and pyrocarving, sculpting, and more. What keeps me going is the music in each gourd, the challenge and the miracle of what gourds offer. I am fascinated with the possibilities and am a slave to the gourd.

In 2005, I founded the Wisconsin Gourd Society. Soon after, I began exhibiting in galleries: Overture Center for the Arts Gallery (Madison, Wisconsin), Madison Museum of Contemporary Art, Frehner Gallery in Monroe, Wisconsin, Longbranch Gallery in Mineral Point and at the Madison Arts Board. In 2009 I was awarded the People's Choice award at the Art By The Stream fine arts festival in Boscobel, Wisconsin. I currently teach gourd art throughout the Midwest and still hear the music in every gourd.

I live in Blue Mounds, Wisconsin, with my husband, Larry Haas, known as The Gourd Guy. It is through him that I became acquainted with gourds—he has been a gourd farmer for twenty plus years and is the largest provider of clean, hard shell gourds in Wisconsin. We are blessed with three dogs, Juju, Chester, and Latimer, and our fearless cat, Kittyboohoo.

Cass Schorsch

Cass Schorsch is a master creator and teacher of fiber and bark basket techniques. She discovered her craft twenty-five years ago at a convention and has been hooked ever since. Mostly self-taught in her craft, Cass focuses on multiple techniques in basket weaving. This focus is clear in her works, which expand one's view of what is possible in basketry. Cass looks to Japanese basket weaving, which is especially complex, for her inspiration, as well as to the natural world. Cass has decided to narrow it down to birch bark and a little bit of cedar. The eastern white cedar is harvested from the upper peninsula of Michigan near the Hessel/Cedarville area. All the birch bark is from Vermont as the trees in Michigan have the blight or birch borer disease. Cass's work has been exhibited throughout the United States with a solo exhibit at the Boston Arts and Crafts Society. Her work has also been presented in numerous publications, including 500 Baskets and Weaving History.

Dianne Schuler

Since childhood, Dianne has had her hands in a variety of arts and crafts. She enjoys beading, weaving, papier-mâché sculpture, and working with gourds. For the last ten years, she has been carving, burning, clay sculpting, weaving, and most of all, experimenting with different techniques with her gourd art. She prefers her gourd art to be functional, simple, and as natural as possible. Dianne lives in North Carolina with her husband, Ron.

Laraine E. Short

Laraine's Creative Corner
AGourdPainter@aol.com

Laraine Short is a member of the National Society of Decorative Painters and president of the local chapter, Decorative Artists of Jacksonville. She is also president of the Northeast Florida Gourd Patch and the Florida Gourd Society.

Laraine teaches decorative painting classes at her studio, local and state chapters, art shows, art stores, local and state patches, and state and national conventions. She joined the American Gourd Society and the Florida Gourd Society in 2000. The same year she entered her gourds in competition and won her first blue ribbons for her gourd art. Laraine also received Best of Division in 2003 at the Florida gourd show. She also received blue ribbons at the Alabama, Indiana, North Carolina, and Ohio gourd shows.

Laraine likes painting her own designs and has over fifty pattern packets. In the last couple of years she has added inking, weaving, clay, and burning to her pattern packets. She also has designs in painting books by Quick and Easy Painting, Plaid, and design books by Sterling Publishing, Quick and Easy Gourd Crafts, and Glorious Gourds Decorating. Laraine loves to paint and doesn't feel like her day is complete if she hasn't picked up a paint brush. You might find her in her studio around two or three o'clock in the morning with a paint brush in her hand.

Polly Adams Sutton

http://pollyadamssutton.blogspot.com

Polly Adams Sutton is a full time studio artist, working with cedar bark to create sculptural baskets. Her educational background was art with an emphasis on painting and printmaking. Upon settling in the Pacific Northwest thirty years ago, she discovered basketry and has taught it ever since. She harvests cedar bark each spring in logging areas near Seattle, Washington. Her sculptural work is primarily twined, although she has been experimenting with wire as a woven element in her asymmetrical shapes. She exhibits her work in galleries and is represented at SOFA Chicago by Jane Sauer Gallery. Her work was chosen for the cover illustration of 500 Baskets. Her work is found in Selected Permanent Collections: Racine Art Museum, Racine, Wisconsin, Museum of Fine Arts, Boston, Massachusetts, Michigan State University Museum, East Lansing, Michigan, and Edmonds Art Museum, Edmonds, Washington.

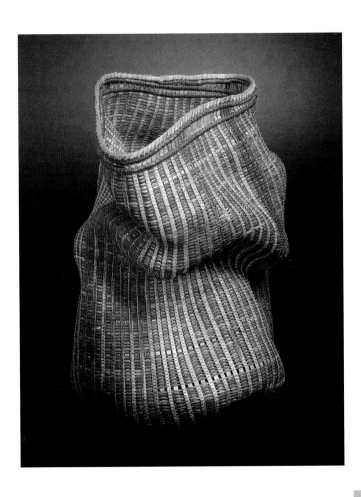

Gerri Swanson

Kelp Kreations
gerrisbaskets@yahoo.com

Gerri (Gairaud) Swanson started coiling pine needles in the early 1980s. Enthralled with the art, she started working with date palm branches, and dying her own raffia. In the late 1980s, she learned to weave and twine with many different types of natural materials, including seagrasses, reeds, willow, palm sheaths, and more. After purchasing a condo on the beach in December 2000, she decided to explore working with kelp. A new passion was born! She continues to work with pine needles and other materials, but her most desired pieces by others are her unique "kelp kreations." She lives on the beach on the Monterey Bay on the coast of California.

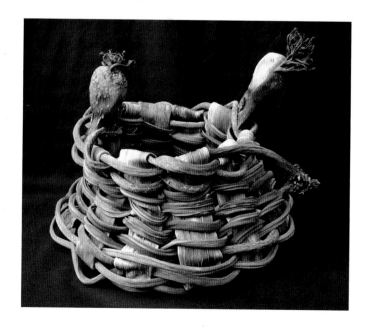

Shirley Thomason

www.shatomabaskets.com.

I've been making pine needle baskets and gourd baskets for over ten years now. I have my own style of basket and gourd art. Because I have Cherokee background, a lot of my gourd baskets tend to have a Native American theme, which comes natural to me. I am known as Shatoma by many and I have used that name for my artwork.

The gourds used are hard shell gourds grown in California, which are very thick and very good to carve and do pyrography on. Because I was a basket maker first, I tend to make gourd baskets using longleaf pine needles from Florida and either silk, raffia or artificial sinew for my threads.

Some of my gourd baskets are in galleries in Arizona, Georgia, and New Hampshire. I have won some ribbons for them at the Texas State Fair and Texas Gourd Society as well. My baskets and gourds are sold in galleries in Arizona, Texas, Georgia, and New Hampshire, and I often sell at local shows in Texas. I also teach gourd and basket making in my hometown, Carrollton, Texas. For many years I sold on Ebay, Etsy, and Shop Handmade, as well as my own website.

Angie Wagner

The County Seat, Inc.
www.countryseat.com

Angie Wagner was raised in a very rural section of Berks County. She continues to live as close to nature as possible. Inspired by the patterns and colors she sees every day, she works to create symmetry and contemporary forms from chaotic natural materials. She grows and harvests many of the accents used in her work, which led to the name Woven Branch Designs. She specializes in round reed work and gourd art, but is always exploring new materials and techniques.

Don Weeke

Don Weeke has been making baskets and gourds for thirty years. The primary focus of his work is form and texture. His work can be seen in numerous publications such as *The Complete Book of Gourd Craft and 500 Baskets*.

Debbie Wilson

Artbasgo

Gourd artist Debbie Wilson lives in the beautiful foothills of the Blue Ridge Mountains. She has taught art for over twenty years, and during that time has found herself a niche in gourd art. By weaving, carving, burning, and embellishing, she transforms gourds into extravagant works of art. Debbie is a member of: Upstate Visual Arts, Trillium Arts, South Carolina Gourd Society, American Gourd Society, Palmetto Gourd Group, Metropolitan Arts Council and Chesnee Artisan Center.

Peggy Wiedemann

Basketry by Peggy Wiedemann
www.peggywiedemann.com

Peggy graduated from the University of California, Los Angeles with a degree in Fine Arts, and a broad interest in expanding her knowledge, skills, and talent. She experimented in a variety of mediums, including oils, pen-and-ink drawing, printmaking, sculpture, and ceramics. In her early years, she introduced art and the creative process to children of all ages as a school teacher. During this time, she also managed an art gallery and was an importer of baskets from a host of countries and cultures. The basket import business exposed her to a variety of cultures, craftsmen, and artists, as well as many forms of materials and techniques. It also enticed her to become an avid collector of Native American and African baskets, and become a basket maker.

As a basket maker, Peggy uses a wide variety of materials. She has a strong preference for natural fibers. She also enjoys personally gathering many of these materials, such as pine needles. To these natural materials, she adds metal, beads, and "found" objects to form unique pieces. The play among mind, hands, and a host of materials continually stimulates the creative process and leads her work in new directions. She has an extensive exhibition history in the United States and Peggy is well represented in museums, galleries, and private collections.

Pamela Zimmerman

www.pamelazimmerman.net

Pamela Zimmerman is a self-taught fiber artist, using mostly basket making techniques, not necessarily in a traditional manner. Pamela previously was a National Park ranger, and lived and worked close to nature. Active in the online weaving community, she is credited with fueling a resurgence in popular interest in learning the coil technique. She founded the website The Pine Needle Group in 1998. She co-founded a weaving guild that focuses on natural fibers and is a board member and web master of the North Carolina Basket Makers' Association. Her work has appeared in many publications and in 2009 she was a Niche Award finalist. She has been asked to join the faculty of the National Basketry Organizations' Traditions and Innovations in Basketry VI.

Bibliography

Books

Campbell-Amsler, Jo. *Nature's Embellishments.* Monticello, Iowa: Willow Ridge Press, 1993.

Daughtery, Robin T. *Splint Woven Basketry.* Loveland, Colorado: Interweave Press, 1986.

Devine, Catherine. *Coiled Designs for Gourd Art.* Atglen, Pennsylvania: Schiffer, 2008.

Gillooly, Maryanne. *Natural Baskets.* Pownal, Vermont: Storey Communications, Inc., 1992.

Kieffer, Susan Mowery, editor, *500 Baskets.* New York, New York: Sterling Publishing, 2006.

La Ferla, Jane. *Making Creative Baskets.* New York, New York: Sterling Publishing, 2000.

Lumpkin, Beryl Omega. *From Vines to Vessels: A Vine Gatherer's Handbook.* Johnson City, Tennessee: The Overmountain Press, 1987.

Shaw, Robert. *American Buskets.* New York, New York: Clarkson/Potter Publishers, 2000.

Siler, Lyn. *Handmade Baskets.* New York, New York: Sterling Publishing Co., Inc., 1992.

_____. *The Basket Book.* New York, New York: Sterling Publishing Co., Inc., 1988.

Sloan, Betsey. *Antler Art for Baskets and Gourds.* Atglen, Pennsylvania: Schiffer, 2011.

Stewart, Hilary. *Cedar.* Vancouver, British Columbia: Douglas & McIntyre Ltd., 1984.

Sudduth, Billie Ruth. *Baskets A Book for Makers and Collectors.* Madison, Wisconsin: Handbooks Press, 1999.

Summit, Ginger. *Gourds in Your Garden.* New York, New York: Sterling Publishing Co., Inc., 1998.

Summit, Ginger. *Gourd Crafts.* New York, New York: Sterling Publishing Co., Inc., 2000.

Web Sites

American Gourd Society
www.americangourdsociety.org

BasketMakers.com
Description: A comprehensive informational site for basket makers, basket artists, vendors of basket making materials, and all others interested in the art of basketry.
Contact: Susi Nuss
http://basketmakers.com

Basket Making
www.basket-making.com

Craft Revival
www.wcu.edu/craftrevival

Mississippi State University/ Rivercane
www.rivercane.msstate.edu

Nantucket Lightship Museum
www.nantucketlightshipbasketmuseum.org/index.html

NativeTech: Native American Technology & Art
www.nativetech.org/plants/sweetgrass.html

Natural Fibers Group
http://naturalfibersgroup.tripod.com
www.nativetech.org

Pine Needles Group
www.pineneedlegroup.com

Surrounded by Beauty
www.artsmia.org/surrounded-by-beauty/index.html

Tree and Traditions
www.umaine.edu/hudsonmuseum/tree2.htm

Wayne Mattox Antiques and Auctions
www.antiquetalk.com/columns/column264.html

Western Carolina University/ Rivercane Studies
www.wcu.edu/24629.asp

Wikipedia: The Free Encyclopedia
http://en.wikipedia.org

There are many wonderful basket and gourd suppliers. If you need a specific material, check with Susi Nuss. She has a site called basket makers (http://basketmakers.com/). You will find sources for baskets and gourds. You will also find contact information for basket and gourd organizations. The following is a list of the suppliers I use for most of my gourd and basket supplies.

Amish Gourds
P.O. Box 21972
York, PA 17402
Phone toll-free: 877-843-0770
www.amishgourds.com

Arnie's Arts 'n Crafts
3741 W Houghton Lake Drive
Houghton Lake, Michigan 48629
Customer Support/Phone Orders 1-800-563-2356
www.baskctpatterns.com

Artistic wire
www.artisticwire.com

Aurora Creations
(Good source for the shave horse)
Elaine Robson of Greer, SC
www.aurorabaskets.com/index.htm

B. Toucan, Inc.
(good source for hemp, waxed lined thread)
www.btoucan.com

Bamboo Poles Shop and Haiku Bamboo Nursery
Contact: Stefani Oshima
Phone: (828) 685-3053
Email: stefanioshima@hotmail.com

Basket, Beads, and Threads
Judy Wilson
www.judykwilson.com/title/Page_1x.html

Basket Weaving.Com
www.basketweavingsupplies.com

Bayou Gourd Farm
www.bayougourds.com
318-445-3969

BeadedLily
www.beadedlily.com

Blue Whale Arts
www.bluewhalearts.com
603-679-1961

Bonnie Gibson's Arizona Gourds
www.arizonagourds.com

Botanical Booty
Eve Elliott
evelliott@yahoo.com
http://botanicalbooty.blogspot.com

Claw, Antler & Hide Company
735 Mount Rushmore Road
Custer, SD 57730
www.clawantlerhide.com

Dancing Cedar Arts
336 Glenns Valley Road
Sequim, WA 98382
www.dancingcedararts.com

Earth Guild
33 Haywood Street
Asheville NC 28801
1-800-327-8448
http://earthguild.com

East Troy Basketry
2082 Church Street
P.O. Box 643
East Troy, WI 53120
Toll Free: (888) 424-9866
www.easttroybasketry.com

Eidnes Furs, Inc.
83363 Hwy 3 South
St. Maries, ID 83861-7175
(208) 245-4753
www.eidnesfurs.com

Fernsink Gourds
www.fernsinkgourds.com
352-493-1534

Florida Pine Needles
Barb Nelson
www.artgalstudio.etsy.com
artgal@mindspring.com

Frank's Cane and Rush Supply
7252 Heil Avenue
Huntington Beach, CA 92647
Phone: (714) 847-0707
Fax: (714) 843-5645
Email: mfrank@franksupply.com

Frantic Stamper, Inc.
www.franticstamper.com

Gimplace.Com
www.gimplace.com/

Ghost Creek Gourds
Dickie and Linda Martin, 2108 Ghost Creek Road,
Laurens, SC 29360
864-682-5251
www.ghostcreekgourds.com

Gratiot Lake Basketry
5484 Petermann Lane
Mohawk, MI 49950-9612
www.gratiotlakebasketry.com/

Greg Leiser Farms
www.GourdFarmer.com
530-735-6677

Grip-All Jaws
P.O. Box 55
McCleart, WA 98557

H.H. Perkins Co.
http://hhperkins.com

Lena Braswell's Gourd Farm
Rt. 1, Box 73, Wrens, Georgia 30833
1-706-547-6784

Nate's Nantuckets, Inc.
17 Waterloo Street
Warner, NH 03278
www.basketshop.com/

Onno Besier
(source for gourd cleaning tools)
1-912-772-3911

Primitive Originals
344 Creekside Drive, Leesburg, GA 31763
229-420-9982
www.primitiveoriginals.com/

Pumpkin Hollow, LLC
Darrell and Ellen Dalton, Owners
671 CR 336
Piggott, AR 72454
Phone (870) 598-3568
www.pumpkinhollow.com/index.html

Redwood City Seed Company/Sweetgrass
Box 361, Redwood City, CA 94064
Phone (650) 325-7333
http://userwebs.batnet.com/rwc-seed/sweetgrass.html

Royalwood, Ltd.
517 Woodville Rd., Mansfield, OH 44907
Phone: 1-419-526-1630 or
1-800-526-1630 (toll free)
www.royalwoodltd.com

Sandylady's Gourd Farm
Email: sandlady@sandlady.com
www.sandlady.com/

Sawdust Connections, LLC
www.GourdSupplies.com
505-506-3558

Smucker's Gourd Farm
317 Springfield Road
Kinzer, PA 17535
717-354-6118

Suzanne Moore's N.C. Basket Works
130 Main Street, P.O. Box 744
Vass, NC 28394
1- 800-338-4972
www.ncbasketworks.com

The Basket Maker's Catalog
Phone: 1-800-447-7008
www.basketmakerscatalog.com

The Basketry Studio
(good source for cedar bark)
281 Mantle Road, Sequim, WA 98382
1-360-683-0050
www.thebasketrystudio.com/supplies

The Caning Shop
Contact: Jim Widess
Phone: 1.800.544.3373
Email: jim@caning.com
www.caning.com

The Country Seat, Inc.
Contact: Donna or Angie
Phone: 610-756-6124
Email: ctryseat@fast.net
www.countryseat.com

The Gourd Pile
874 Morrison Road, P.O. Box 516
Morven, GA 31638
229-775-2123

The Pod Lady
Betsey Sloan
828-349-0941 (please call prior to 8 p.m.)
betseysloan@yahoo.com
www.thepodlady.com/

The Wicker Woman ®
1250 Highway 25
Angora, MN, USA 55703
www.wickerwoman.com/contact-us

Tom Keller Gourds
www.tomkellergourds.com
662-494-3334

Tubular Wire Mesh Ribbon
http://tubularwiremeshribbon.com/

Turkey Branch Gourds
C.L. & Willene Arnsdorff
Springfield, GA
912-754-3779

Turtle Feathers
PO Box 1307, Bryson City, North Carolina 28713
1-828.488.8586
www.turtlefeathers.net

Welburn Gourd Farm
40635-D De Luz Rd., Fallbrook, CA 92028
1-877-420-2613
www.welburngourdfarm.com

Windstream
arnsdorffw@windstream.net

Wuertz Gourd Farm
2487 E. Highway 287, Casa Grande, Arizona, 85194,
1-520-723-4432
www.wuertzfarm.com/index.html

Border: The top edge of the basket that keeps the basket together. It is also called the rim.

Cane: The outer peel of the rattan plant.

Cedar: Type of conifer in the cypress family. The inner bark of the red and yellow cedar tree is used for weaving.

Coil: A reed coil wound up in a circle.

Cordage: A term used for any type of rope or string made by twisting fibers together.

Embellishment: Decorating your basket or gourd with natural and manmade elements.

Girdle: To kill a tree or woody shrub by removing or destroying a band of bark and cambium from its circumference.

Gourds: Cucurbits, members of the cucurbitaceous family and this fruit grows on vines.

Hackle: To chop roughly.

Hairs: Splinters and feathering of the reed that can be eliminated by cutting or singeing.

Hard-shell gourds: Member of the Lagenaria and used for ornamentation, crafting, vessels, and general interest.

Holdfast: Root systems.

Jacaranda pod: The fruit from the sub-tropical tree native to South America that has been widely planted elsewhere because of its beautiful and long-lasting blue flowers. The pods are used as embellishments.

Loppers: A type of scissors used for pruning twigs and small branches.

Nantucket: Sturdy functional baskets that originated more than 150 years ago by the whaling crew manning the lightships off the coast of Nantucket Island, Massachusetts. The baskets are usually made with cane over wooden molds.

Philodendron: A large, semi-woody shrub with enormous glossy leaves. The sheath is used for embellishment for gourds and baskets.

Plait: To form by interlaying interweaving; to braid; to plait.

Pyrography: The craft of decorating wood, leather, or gourds with heated tools.

Rattan: A vine-like palm usually found in tropical areas of Asia.

Reed: Flexible strands cut from the core of rattan and used for weaving.

Retted: A process employing the action of micro-organisms and moisture on plants to dissolve or rot away much of the cellular tissue.

Rib Basket: A vessel made of osiers or other twigs, cane, rushes, splints, or other flexible material that has ribs and is woven with other materials.

River cane: Plant that grows by the river and needs much moisture. The Cherokee used it to weave twill woven baskets.

Row: This is when the weaver goes completely around the basket.

Sisal: An agave (succulent plant) that has stiff fibers used to make twine and rope.

Spathe: A modified or specialized leaf that forms a sheath to encase the flower cluster of certain plants such as palms.

Spiral: A design formed with twills or waling, using a continuous weave.

Spokes: Material that forms the rigid frame for weaving a basket.

Stipe: A stalk that supports some other structure in a plant.

Stook: A heap or bundle; a truss of flax or of sheaves of grain.

Sweet grass: Sweet smelling grass native to the southeastern United States, It is used to weave baskets. Another variety grows in the Northeast and Northwest.

Tines: A branch of a deer's antlers.

Triple twine: Three rod waling where you are using three pieces of reed to twine.

Twill: A weaving technique going over and under different number of spokes and the design steps up each row.

Twine: Weaving technique also called pairing that uses two weavers, which twist around the spokes.

Upsett: To "upsett" means to gently bend up the spokes at the base perimeters. This just makes the upward weaving easier.

Wale: Pattern in weaving where the left weaver in a set (three, four...) goes over two spokes and behind one.

Weaver: Flexible round or flat material used for weaving.

Notes

Notes

Notes

Notes

Notes